248.4
W799f

Sherwood E. Wirt

1 John 3:23

D0021314

CHRISTIAN HERITAGE COLLEGE

SAN DIEGO, CALIFORNIA 1970

CHRISTIAN
HERITAGE
COLLEGE
LIBRARY

PRESENTED BY

Sherwood Eliot Wirt

248.4   Wirt
W799f   Freshness of the
          spirit

CHRISTIAN HERITAGE COLLEGE
2100 Greenfield Dr.
El Cajon, CA 92021

Freshness of the Spirit

OTHER BOOKS BY SHERWOOD ELIOT WIRT

Crusade at the Golden Gate
Open Your Bible
Magnificent Promise
Not Me, God
The Social Conscience of the Evangelical
Passport to Life City
Love Song: A translation of Augustine's Confessions
Jesus Power
Enough and to Spare
Afterglow

with Ruth McKinney
You Can Tell the World: New Directions for Christian Writers
Getting into Print

Edited
Spiritual Awakening
The Quiet Corner

with Charlene Anderson
God, I Like You

with Viola Blake
Great Preaching

with Kersten Beckstrom
Living Quotations for Christians

Freshness of the Spirit

SHERWOOD ELIOT WIRT

Published in San Francisco by Harper & Row, Publishers

New York, Hagerstown, San Francisco, London

FRESHNESS OF THE SPIRIT. Copyright © 1978 by Sherwood Eliot Wirt. All rights reserved. Printed in the United States of America. No part of this book may be used or reproduced in any manner whatsoever without written permission except in the case of brief quotations embodied in critical articles and reviews. For information address Harper & Row, Publishers, Inc., 10 East 53rd Street, New York, N.Y. 10022. Published simultaneously in Canada by Fitzhenry & Whiteside Limited, Toronto.

FIRST EDITION

Designed by Jim Mennick

Library of Congress Cataloging in Publication Data
Wirt, Sherwood Eliot.
  FRESHNESS OF THE SPIRIT.

  1. Christian life—1960-   2. Holy Spirit.
3. Wirt, Sherwood Eliot. I. Title.
BV4501.2.W57 1978   248'.4   77-20442
ISBN 0-06-069604-4

78 79 80 81 82 10 9 8 7 6 5 4 3 2 1

To my grandson Tyler Eliot Wirt

33482

Contents

Foreword

by Malcolm Muggeridge

HERE in this book we have an account of a man's quest for God. It is a theme that has been endlessly explored and that will go on preoccupying minds that are venturesome and curious till the end of time. Ultimately, it is all there is to think about, write about, be concerned about, live and die about. It comprehends everything, while recognizing that everything, in our mortal terms, is nothing; it starts nowhere, and can never in this world reach a definitive destination; and although each individual traveler covers new ground and, wide-eyed, sees new wonders, it is the same. As John Donne puts it in his *Progress of the Soul*, itself an essay in the genre:

> For though through many straits and lands I roam,
> I launch at Paradise, and I sail towards home.

The traveler, once started on his spiritual pilgrimage, looks back with distaste on his previous venturings forth; in Sherwood Wirt's case, on the routine activities of a minister—preparing his sermons, organizing the activities of the church in his charge, attending to the needs of his congregation as best he can, and, more recently, editing the magazine *Decision* on

behalf of the Billy Graham Association. No doubt he exagger-
ates his own deficiencies and spiritual deadness, but this, too, is
part of the standard procedure. I used to think there was a
certain affectation in saints, like Francis of Assisi, who insisted
that they were the worst and most degraded of sinners. Later, I
came to understand that it is precisely nearness to God that
intensifies awareness of the appalling disparity between our
poor efforts to love and serve Him and the love and service due
Him. In the same sort of way, climbers of Mount Everest
become overwhelmed by what they have undertaken when
they have climbed high enough to see peak after peak between
them and the summit.

In Sherwood Wirt's case, as he recounts, the change in
direction came as a result of attending, in his journalistic
capacity, a revival meeting in Manitoba, Canada, in mid-
winter. Climatically, it was an inhospitable scene; spiritually, it
profoundly affected him, not so much in the sense that he
became one of the revived as because he was moved and
thrilled by the enactment in contemporary terms of the Apostle
Paul's experience on the Damascus Road. After the routine
pieties of his ministry, suddenly he found himself witnessing
the very process of being born again—as might a butterfly
shaking itself clear of its chrysalis and getting ready to fly.
Such experiences have been occurring all through the twenty
centuries of Christendom, and there are many accounts of
them, ranging between the testimony of a simple hermit-nun
like Julian of Norwich and that of a brilliant scientist and
polemicist like Blaise Pascal. They all have one characteristic in
common: They speak of a light shining in darkness, order
emerging from chaos, coherence from incoherence, or, as I
have often put it myself in contemporary terms, a film getting
into sync, so that the muzzy picture becomes clear, the con-
fused words make sense, the shapes and movements portrayed
lose their distortion and become natural.

As my own life moves to its close, I increasingly feel that the experience of living, in one's own inner being or historically as part of a collectivity, consists of being confronted with a whole series of parables, which need to be unravelled to reveal their true meaning, the Christian revelation providing the key. Without Christ, that is to say, life has no more meaning than the groups of figures I used to get radioed to me when I was an Intelligence officer in the war; deciphered, with the aid of the codebook, their meaning became clear and they made sense.

Once interpreted, the parables all say essentially the same thing—that in all creation, and in every instant of our existence, truth is within our grasp if only we have eyes to see it, minds to grasp it, and the Holy Spirit to irradiate it. This is Sherwood Wirt's conclusion, as it is the conclusion of every true seeker after God. Looking away from the fantasy of a busy and useful life into God's very eyes, he concludes:

> We used to resent people, envy people, fear people, shun people, even detest and despise people. Now God has filled us with love for them. His perfect love has cast out our fears and our bitterness ... Our lives are flooded with peace and joy, but most of all with love. The same love that caused Jesus Christ to go to the cross for us, and to send us the Spirit of Truth, now motivates us to reach out to others. ... You understand that we had nothing to do with this change except to ask for it ... But God is God, and when He moves, He moves in sovereignty. He sends no envoys or plenipotentiaries, He comes Himself.

Thinking of how I should write this Foreword, I happened to turn to some words of Jean-Pierre Caussade on the necessity for total surrender to God (*L'Abandon*):

> All individual ideas, understanding, endeavour, argument are but a source of fantasy, and when the soul discovers the folly of her own efforts and finally realizes their futility, then it becomes clear to us that God has hidden and obscured every other channel in order to show us how to exist in Him and Him alone.

So, the eighteenth-century Jesuit addressing cloistered nuns and the busy twentieth-century evangelist and editor are at one in the Holy Spirit. If we were to collect together all the others saying the same thing in their different idioms and circumstances, what libraries would be filled with their writings! From St. Augustine to C. S. Lewis, from Thomas Aquinas to Simone Weil, from *The Cloud of Unknowing* to William Blake, from Blaise Pascal to John Henry Newman—I could go on and on; a mighty chorus, enveloped in one Holy Spirit, proclaiming one truth, each individual voice fulfilling Jesus's prophecy, that though heaven and earth should pass away his words would never pass away.

Introduction

APART from the Holy Spirit, the Bible is little more than a pile of disconnected writings surviving from early days in the Mediterranean basin. And apart from the Bible, the Holy Spirit is little more than a vague, confusing, and rather spooky religious notion.

So it is important, if Christianity is to make any sense at all, that we try to learn from the sacred Scripture something about the Person and operation of the Holy Spirit. Many excellent books have been written to explain in detail what the Bible teaches regarding the Spirit of God, but I aspire to no such goal. My purpose is simply to investigate the assertion, which I heard for the first time during the 1971-1972 revival in western Canada, that the Holy Spirit is love.

The fact that I was filled with the Spirit during that revival helps to explain my motivation in writing. But in the six years following my visit to Elim Chapel in Winnipeg, Manitoba, other things began to happen that eventually drew me back to the typewriter.

For one, the New Testament proved to be a rich mine of teaching about the Spirit. I had known about the lode of treasure, but had never found it because I'd been wandering in the stopes. To cite one example, I discovered that in the fourth chapter of the First Letter of John, the apostle sets up for us not one test of the Holy Spirit's Presence, but two.

The well-known test in the second verse is, of course, based upon faith in Jesus Christ: "Every spirit that confesses that Jesus Christ is come in the flesh is of God." But in the seventh verse of that chapter, John poses another test and continues stressing it to the end of the chapter. The test seems to base the Spirit's Presence on our love for each other: "If we love one another, God abides in us, and his love is completed in us. By this we know that we abide in him, and he in us, because he has given to us of his Spirit" (1 John 4:12-13).

John has a way of bringing it all down to me and the way I act.

Another unexpected happening has been the expansion of my ministry. Through the Billy Graham schools of evangelism at the crusades I have been invited to speak to pastors and their wives in many parts of the world about the filling of the Spirit. Churches have written asking to have "Afterglows"—informal prayer gatherings that take place usually after a normal evening service, in which kneeling, laying on of hands, and singing form part of the experience.*

Being with brothers and sisters of many different backgrounds, from Roman Catholic to Pentecostal, and watching their responses has convinced me that much truth lies in what was taught me during the Canadian revival. Since it has proved impossible to dissociate my spiritual viewpoint from the events of that revival, I have described my participation in it in some detail.

I would like to express thanks to my wife Winola, an author, who has listened to many reworkings of the present volume, and to members of a San Diego County critique group

---

*See *Afterglow* (Grand Rapids, Mich.; Zondervan, 1975).

who have offered much help in improving the text. My appreciation also goes to Mr. Muggeridge for his Foreword, and to Miss Kersten Beckstrom for expertly editing and preparing the typescript.

S. E. W.

Poway, California
January 1978

1. Discovering

In the second week of December 1971, a weird letter arrived from my friend Leonard Ravenhill, who writes discerningly on religious subjects. It was postmarked from the Bahamas, but it was all about Canada. Leonard was in a state about the Saskatchewan revival. He had fired off missives to me before— Leonard is a kind of revival prophet—but this one was different.

"When meetings last until after midnight," he wrote, "when couples tear up their divorce papers before a thousand people; when the chief of police says there is a rash of crime confessing; when Simpson-Sears, Ltd., has to open a special account to take care of all the shoplifting being returned by church members; when lawyers, psychologists and priests are being saved; when deacons and church members are broken in spirit; and when this happens night after night for weeks, one might say there is a touch of revival. The city of Saskatoon is shaking under the power of God. Hop a plane, my brother, and get a foretaste of glory divine."

I looked at the calendar. Upper Saskatchewan, in December? Outside my window in Minneapolis, cardboard wise men and angels were dangling above the entrance to the world headquarters of the Billy Graham Evangelistic Association.

It's not easy to win people to Christ during the Christmas season. The weather's against it. Committees don't like to meet. Pastors are apt to find themselves going in circles. Evangelists are aware of the situation, so they stay home like everybody else and watch their kids perform in Sunday School nativity programs.

But here was Ravenhill's letter, giving me orders that seemed to have come from higher up. Various reports had come in earlier of a spiritual eruption of some sort in western Canada. Revival was supposed to have started in a Baptist church in Saskatoon under the leadership of two American evangelists, Ralph and Lou Sutera.

As editor of *Decision* I had decided to pass up the story. My reasoning was that if God wanted to assign me to cover a spiritual awakening in Billy Graham's magazine, he would have the foresight to launch it under the auspices of the Billy Graham Association.

Now I was in a quandary. What had caused Leonard to write as he did? Was God really behind it? How would I answer this letter? I reached for the telephone and dialed Ebenezer Baptist Church, Saskatoon.

"Is the pastor there?"

"No, Mr. McLeod has taken a leave of absence from the church."

"Can you tell me where he is?"

"He is in Winnipeg."

"Oh. Is a revival going on up there?"

"Yes, we have had a revival."

"Oh. And is it going on now?"

"Yes. In Winnipeg."

Winnipeg! Only one stop from Minneapolis on Northwest

Airlines. I placed a call to our Winnipeg Billy Graham office. Gertrude Adrian, the manager, answered.

"What's this about a revival?" I asked.

"You know, that's funny," she said. "I've been revived. Last night."

"I'm coming up," I said. "Can you get me a motel room?"

On Wednesday afternoon, December 15, I arrived at the Winnipeg airport and was met by Gertrude.

"You're to dine with Don and Fred," she said. I was pleased. They were members of Billy Graham's Canadian board.

Upon reaching the office I began putting in some local calls. The first was to a Minneapolis pastor who was now preaching in Winnipeg. "What's this about revival?" I asked.

"We're not in it," he said.

Next, I called the city desk of a Winnipeg newspaper, the *Free Press*. A young woman answered. "Are you aware," I asked, "that a revival has broken out in your city, just like the one in Saskatoon a few weeks ago?"

A pause. "What is revival?" she asked.

That evening at dinner I mentioned the reason for my visit to my board member friends. Revival? In Winnipeg? It was news to them. But they obligingly dropped me off at Elim Chapel after dinner and I walked into a service that changed me forever.

LEOPARD SPOTS

As a teenager living in Berkeley, California, I used to go on Sunday nights to an amusement park in Alameda called Neptune Beach. There some of us would head for the "ring the bell" concession, pay our dimes, and wait our turn at the mallet. The aim was to strike a blow that would send the little weight upward; if it hit the top we would win a kewpie doll.

Being a lightweight, I never had what it took to make that bell ring at the top. And that became the story of my life; no kewpie dolls.

Ten years later, after graduating from the University of California and working as a professional newspaperman, I threw away my mallet and entered the Christian ministry, hoping to find a somewhat different atmosphere from the world I knew. It was different, all right, but not all that different; so eventually I retrieved my mallet.

The December night in 1971 when I walked into Winnipeg's Elim Chapel I had my mallet with me. It was a cassette recorder; if this was a heaven-sent revival, I intended to bring it down to earth.

The first thing God did was to make the batteries in that recorder run down; and they were new batteries too.

The church was packed. A seat was found for me in the front row. The song leader was directing the congregation in some robust choruses I had never heard before—"Heavenly Father, I Appreciate You," "Jesus Sets Me Absolutely Free," and "We'll Give the Glory to Jesus." Then he said, "If anyone has been revived in the last twenty-four hours, come up here and tell us about it."

The last twenty-four hours?

But there they were, lined up on both sides of the platform. One, a young man named Jake, said, "Last Saturday I prayed all the way to the meeting that I'd get a flat tire so I wouldn't have to go. Afterward it seemed as if a 200-pound sack of flour had been lifted off my back."

Another, named Ray, said, "Last night I did what I've known for the past fifteen years that I'd have to do some day."

A married couple followed them and told how their twenty-year marriage had been at the breaking point when they walked forward the previous Friday. The wife said she had decided to take the two youngest of their six children, go back to her parents in Vancouver, and look for a job. The husband was planning to see a psychiatrist.

When they reached the front of the church, they said, many others were already there, and not enough counselors were available. For half an hour they knelt with no one to talk to but each other. For the first time in years they began to communicate, to relate, and to discuss what they were doing to each other. By the time the counselor got there, they didn't need him. The Holy Spirit had been their counselor, and the marriage was healed.

"God took a divine solvent," said the woman, whose name was Evelyn, "and dissolved all the bitterness I had stored up against my husband over the years. Harry and I have fallen in love all over again."

Well, now. But my recorder was acting up and I was in a bad mood. All eyes were fixed on the preacher, the Reverend Wilbert L. McLeod, a man in his early fifties. Underneath his coat I spotted a cardigan, and whoever heard of an evangelist preaching in a sweater?

His text was from Jeremiah 13:23, "Can the leopard change his spots?" and he was talking about change. There was much quoting of Scripture, yet the message was brief, which in itself surprised me. Most people, he was saying, think they cannot change, so they settle for something less. It's true that spots are spots; but what man cannot do, God can do.

I had heard it all before, and now we were into the closing hymn. No invitation was given, yet people began coming out of the woodwork and swarming to the front. I couldn't believe it. They moved me from my front seat to the second row, with all my electronic claptrap. Then to the third row.

"We need counselors," Mr. McLeod was saying, "but I don't

care if you have taught Sunday School for thirty years—if you haven't been revived, don't come down here. Because these people have been revived."

I didn't volunteer.

Suddenly it was over, and Gertrude was at the back, waiting for me. "Come on," she said. "We're walking over to my church for the Afterglow."

"Walking? How far is it?"

"About a quarter of a mile."

It was zero outside.

A COLD SWEAT

The Afterglow circle went on and on, punctuated by testimonies, requests for prayer, choruses, and verses of Scripture.

I had never seen anything like it. The air was electric with expectation. A group of young people left and came back. People slipped out of the social hall and knelt for prayer in niches and corners of the church. They returned tear-stained and smiling.

As a Christian I was glad to see them getting help with their problems. Never for a moment did it occur to me that I, too, had a problem and that my heart needed revival.

Seated a few chairs away from me was the couple named Harry and Evelyn. On my reporter's pad I scribbled a note to them: "Would you come to Minneapolis and share your testimony with some of our church people?"

The note came back: "We're willing to do whatever the Lord wants us to do."

I stared at the writing. The Lord? I hadn't asked him about it. It just seemed like a good idea. Whatever I thought the church needed, I assumed, automatically carried the stamp of divine approval.

At midnight Gertrude said, "Tomorrow is a working day.

I'm going home. You can stay; I've arranged a ride for you."

An hour and a half later I decided to leave. Only a few people remained, and they were kneeling around a young man with long blond hair. Their hands were laid on him, and they were praying for him.

So this was an Afterglow!

The flight home was a bumpy one—internally. The malfunctioning tape recorder offered no serious problem; I had the story. What was beginning to trouble me was my inviting those foreigners to our city. What was I trying to prove? How did I know they were genuine? Who would pay their way? Why had I stuck out my neck? What were my real motives?

It could be said that I acted on a good impulse, and was merely trying to spread the blessing. That's what Christians are supposed to do, isn't it? A harmless enough activity—unless, of course, one is trespassing on holy ground. Was it not Jacob who said at Bethel, "Surely the Lord is in this place"? (Gen. 28:16).*

As we lifted off the frozen runway, the issues came into sharper relief. I was certain that what I had witnessed in Winnipeg's Elim Chapel was genuine revival sent by God. That itself marked a change in my viewpoint, for I had thought that the age of revivals was over and finished—killed by television. It had seemed to me that a zoom camera would shoot down any future spiritual outbreak before it could get off the ground.

In my book the last genuine awakening took place in the islands of Scotland's Outer Hebrides in 1949-1950.

But even if by a miracle revival were to come in our day, common sense told me that it would hardly begin in western Canada. I imagined that a more likely spot, temperamentally

---

* Where the Revised Standard Version (RSV) or some other recent translation of the Bible is used in this volume, it is so indicated. Where no reference appears, the translation is either from the Authorized (King James) Version, or is the author's direct translation from the Greek text.

speaking, might be Mexico, or Liberia, or the Solomon Islands, or almost anywhere else.

Now all that was out the window. The absence in Winnipeg of evangelistic tricks, media promotion, gimmickry, unusual phenomena, or whipped-up excitement convinced me. So if human effort was not responsible for what I saw taking place, then it must have been of God.

What, then, in God's name, was I doing trying to lure his servants across the border? Did I presume to think God could not bring his revival into the United States without my help? Did he need a by-your-leave from me?

Or was I, in my sly way, trying to slip in a footnote to church history? Was this a ploy to immortalize my name as the Great Importer of the Holy Spirit, the Man God Used to Internationalize the Canadian Revival, the Humble Instrument of the Third (or Fourth, or Fifth) Great Awakening? Half a page, perhaps, in J. Edwin's Orr's next volume on the history of evangelical movements?

You may brand such soliloquizing as dumb, if not pathological, but on that plane I was in a cold sweat, and it wasn't due to cabin temperatures. It came to me that there are no eminences to which human pride does not aspire. The wife of Zebedee had nothing on me.

As our flight crossed into Minnesota, I reflected on the fact that my life story had been a saga of self-promotion. When I wasn't pushing my own cause, it was the cause of my family, or my church, or my organization. Directly or indirectly my goal was the upgrading of Number One.

Good old Woody. Humble, modest, unassuming, self-effacing, meek, shunning the limelight. But right there when the credits were to be handed out. Got the image?

Even when I witnessed to my faith in Jesus Christ I saw that I was consciously or unconsciously promoting myself. Others were more aware of it than I, which is why they sometimes reacted toward me with unfriendly overtones. But those who got in my way I did not think of as my enemies; I looked upon them as enemies of Christ.

It's a dangerous business, trying to help oneself and calling it helping the Lord. One is liable to be caught in the flywheel. I thought about the Old Testament story of a man named Uzzah who was guiding the ark of God as oxen were hauling it toward Jerusalem. The record says that he put out his hand to steady it, and was struck dead.

By the time we landed at Minneapolis-St. Paul International Airport I was in a state of spiritual shock, so much so that I wanted nothing to do with the Canadian revival. It belonged to God; let him handle it.

"We are willing to do whatever the Lord wants us to," Harry and Evelyn had written. Well, let 'em. I refused to psych myself into thinking that the Lord had told me what to do about Winnipeg. It was too late for that. I'd had a good idea, but this wasn't it. I would report what I had seen in the columns of my magazine, and that would be the end of it.

But I hadn't counted on one thing.

THE HAZELNUT

A minister used to drive his car to the town depot each day and sit and watch as the noon empress train went past. People asked him, "Why do you do it?"

He explained, "That train is the only thing going through this town that I don't have to push."

Some pastor friends in the Twin Cities had known about my visit to the Winnipeg revival, and after my return they dropped in to see me. I had vowed that I was through pushing and promoting any and all things of God, and would certainly make no telephone calls or do anything else about the Winni-peg revival. But when my friends began asking me questions, what could I do?

I shared the testimony of Harry and Evelyn, together with my misgivings about inviting them to Minnesota. My pastor friends seemed to think I was touched in the head.

"Bring them down," they said. "We'll use them in our pulpits, and that will help pay the air fare."

So it was that on Sunday, January 9, 1972 this gentle Mennonite pair from Manitoba, Harry and Evelyn Thiessen, told their story of rekindled love in four different Minneapolis churches and conducted an Afterglow that evening. Then they returned home. But in their wake they left a number of Christians newly filled with the Spirit; and I was one of them.

I like to recall those two dedicated people as they stood that day, occasionally wiping their eyes, speaking about the Holy Spirit as someone close and present. Harry was a bearded civil engineer; Evelyn was a mother of six growing children. They knew their Bible and they knew their Lord.

I was a needy person with a deep-seated problem and they ministered to me in love. They forced me to look beyond my pride and ambition to the rancor in my soul and the fundamen-tal discontent of my life. The operant prayer here was for a regenerated but disordered disciple. They interceded and were heard; I asked and was healed.

Nothing happened immediately, but gradually, the first effects began to be felt at home. My wife Winola had not been at the meeting with the Thiessens, but she was more than ready for any improvement in our family situation. As time went on, a kind of greening took place; a new dimension of love penetrated the premises. We began to appreciate and enjoy each other's company in a fresh way. Other family relation-ships were also improved.

The Thiessens and the Wirts are only two families. What

happed to us happened also in different ways to the McLeods, the Derksens, the Willemses, the Sailors, the Teichrobs, the Rachars, the Lutzers, the Boldts, the Whites, and hundreds of other Canadian and American families. In the years that followed, lives were touched in many other parts of the world—in Taiwan, Hong Kong, South Africa, Brazil—and it's still going on.

Some of these people took their testimony to Holland, some to Denmark, some to Argentina. Ralph and Lou Sutera, the identical-twin evangelists, continued their revival ministry both in the United States and in Canada with remarkable spiritual results. It is one of the refreshing stories of the twentieth century.

A day may come when someone will visit the towns and cities of the provinces of western Canada and do some in-depth reporting of what took place under the leading of God's Spirit in 1971 and 1972. I have a feeling that many a story is waiting to be told in the churches of Red Deer, Whitewood, Moose Jaw, Swift Current, Three Hills, Thunder Bay, Prince George, Coquitlam, Dauphin, Brandon, Killam, Abbotsford—to say nothing of Vancouver, Regina, Edmonton, Calgary and Saskatoon. Meanwhile books have been written* and the Canadian Revival Fellowship continues a fruitful ministry.

My contact with God's special season of refreshing in Canada was fleeting, but the reorientation of my ideas about the Church of Jesus Christ was total. To begin with I faced up to my own problem, which was bitterness and lack of love. I asked the Lord to crucify me and to fill me with his Holy Spirit, and thanked him in advance for doing it. If it be pointed out that I could not have become a Christian in the first instance without the Holy Spirit, I will agree heartily; I am no theolo-

---

* I particularly recommend Erwin Lutzer's *Flames of Freedom* (Chicago: Moody, 1976).

gian, but one does not have to study theology to know that you cannot at the same time be filled with the Holy Spirit and filled with resentment, bitterness, and hate.

I was like the man who had to be touched twice by Jesus before he could pass from blindness to clear vision. The first time Jesus touched him, he reported things out of focus; he could only see "men as trees, walking" (Mark 8:24). In my case it was my own life that I failed to bring into sharp definition.

In January 1972, the Holy Spirit became the most important person in my universe instead of the most neglected. He did not supersede Jesus Christ because his only mission is to glorify Jesus Christ. He gave me a new awareness of Jesus, a new understanding of his cross, a new appreciation for the Bible—and a fresh capacity to love. And he took away my mallet forever.

In her "Revelations of Divine Love," a fourteenth-century Christian nun of Norwich, England, known as Lady Julian, wrote, "God showed me a little thing the size of a hazelnut in the palm of my hand, and I thought, 'What may this be?' and was answered, 'It is the universe.' "* It seemed to me, after praying with Harry and Evelyn, that my universe had come together for the first time so that I could look at it as if it were a hazelnut and understand its meaning and God's purpose for it.

I learned that one of the reasons Jesus went to the cross was to send us the Holy Spirit. And I found out one other thing. I discovered why the New Testament was written.

THE PICKLING BARREL

A man in South Dakota told me once during an Afterglow that he loved God so much he was ready to choke anyone who dared speak a work against him.

---

* *Sixteen Revelations of Divine Love,* ed. Roger Hudleston (London: Orchard Books, 1927), p. 9.

I have preached in churches whose members regularly slipped out the side door after the service so they wouldn't have to shake hands with the minister.

In Europe they will show you a hundred tragic sites where Christians expressed their violent disapproval of each other.

Unless I am misreading the signs, a dimension seems to be missing from our practice of the Christian faith. And when I study the early church I find it was often missing there too. And that is why the New Testament was written: to get Christians to love each other.

It wasn't written to get people to love Jesus. Remember, most of the New Testament was addressed to Christians, people who already loved Jesus.

And it was not written primarily to tell people that Jesus loved them. They had already heard that, and most of them believed it.

Nor was it written to reveal God's great love for the human race; they knew about that too.

Actually, only a small part of the New Testament was written evangelistically, aimed at sinners for the purpose of rescuing them from the brink of hell. Some passages in the book of Acts fit that description, as do some of the teachings of Jesus. But the Gospels and letters were not composed to save the human race, or lift the moral tone, or weave the social fabric, or establish rules for civilized living, or promote the spread of the church. Nothing like that!

The New Testament was written primarily to get Christians into a loving relationship with other Christians. Jesus knew that unless and until that happened, nothing would happen; but once it did take place, all the other things would come along. So he said, "Seek ye first the Kingdom" (Matt 6:33). The Kingdom of what? The Kingdom of love, what else?

On Sunday mornings millions of us are taught that God is love and that the Holy Spirit is God. But for some reason the syllogism is not completed; we are not told that the Holy Spirit is love.

We're taught that the Spirit is our Comforter, Convicter, and Enabler; that he is Grace, Power, Wisdom, Truth, Wind, Fire, and Unction. We're told that in the name of Jesus he baptizes believers, anoints them, fills, indwells, seals, witnesses to, teaches, and guides them. We're taught that he dispenses special gifts and produces lasting fruit.

But we are not told that the message of the New Testament is from first to last that the Holy Spirit is love, and that to be filled with the Spirit is to be filled with love, *nothing more and nothing less.*

We enjoy singing the chorus, "I love Jesus because he first loved me." That takes care of the vertical. We also sing, "God so loved the world." That takes care of the sides of the triangle. But what about the base? What about our love for each other?

We Christians have all the riches of God's storehouse to draw from; but when we don't love, we have nothing. The Apostle John wrote, "Beloved, if God so loved us, we ought to love one another" (1 John 4:11). Too many of us have never made that connection. It took me sixty years to make it. For many of those years, as a Christian minister, I tried just about everything else imaginable in my struggle to win a kewpie doll.

Only my mother-in-law said to me, "Sherwood, don't do anything. Let the Spirit do it." It sounded like an insipid idea at the time, but not any more.

In Manitoba they told me that if Christians are not revived, they are "pickling." I've been thinking about that one.

How much love is there in a pickling barrel?

HISTORY LESSON

At this point something tells me I'm wrong. I have to be wrong—think of all that church history, all those century-long debates and quarrels about the Holy Spirit. But that's just the trouble. In going through church history I have been looking for love, and having a rough time finding it.

The New Testament is clear, of course; the words come right from our Lord's mouth. We are to love each other. We're to love even our enemies. We're to bless those who curse us, do good to those who hate us, and pray for those who despitefully use and persecute us.

You inform me that you're nice to people who are nice to you? Big deal. Jesus says you don't have to be a believer to act that way—that's what everybody does. Didn't the great leaders of the church in the past understand that? Of course they did. They knew their Bibles better than I know mine.

Well, then, what happened?

I don't know. When I read John Calvin's *Institutes of the Christian Religion,* my mind boggles at the range of the man's thought, his erudition, his perception. Certainly he is saying the right things: for example, "Let a man be what he may, he is still to be loved, because God is loved." In other words, the love we have for God must be, in Calvin's words, "diffused among all mankind." That's scriptural enough and handsomely expressed. I am an admirer of Calvin.

Did Calvin understand that the Holy Spirit is Love? He calls him a Fountain, the Hand, Water, Oil, Fire, Spirit of Adoption, Life Because of Righteousness. But Love?

Unless we are filled with the Spirit, the same Spirit who filled Jesus, we are simply unable to do what Jesus told us to do. But once we have received the promise of the Father, and the love of God has been poured out in our hearts by the Holy Spirit, then the Spirit does it all by supernatural impartation.

Jesus knew this. He knew I would never be able to love everybody. Some hot-rodder tailgates me, and the next thing I know, I'm on the receiving end of a bumper thumper. Now what? I'm supposed to pull over and say to this driver, "I love you"?

Don't be ridiculous.

That's why Jesus told his followers, "I will ask the Father, and he will give you another Paraclete" (John 14:16). The Greek word *Paraclete* means literally one who is called alongside, one who stands by you, backs you, encourages you, takes your part, comforts you, speaks for you, represents you. He does something for you that you can't do for yourself—just as Jesus did on the cross. The *Paraclete* is the Holy Spirit. He supplies the love I can't muster. He fills me with love and loves through me.

Some people have said to me, "It's all very well for you to rattle on the way you do about love, but you haven't been treated the way I have."

I answer, "Perhaps I haven't, but I did have a lot of bitterness in my heart, and it's gone."

They respond, "Yes, but you haven't been insulted, you haven't been cheated, you haven't been neglected, humiliated, betrayed."

I reply, "No, I guess not, but Jesus was, and he still loved. And Paul and Stephen were, and they still loved." Today in Cambodia and Czechoslovakia and Mozambique, Christians are suffering for Jesus' sake, and they still love. I used to think it was a pose. Now I am convinced it is the Holy Spirit.

My friend Festo Kivengere, Anglican bishop of Kigezi, Uganda, managed to escape with his wife across the border into Rwanda after the assassination of his colleague, Archbishop Janani Luwum, in early 1977. When describing his experience, Bishop Kivengere began with the words, "I love Idi Amin." Idi Amin is the ruler who arranged the murder. How could Festo Kivengere use those words about a man whose actions have repelled so much of the world? The answer is that Bishop Kivengere is a product of the East Africa revival. He is a Spirit-filled man.

Calvin spends 458 brilliant pages talking about the knowledge of God; but he neglects to quote the Apostle John, who says we can never, never, never know God unless we love each other. John asks why we think we can love someone we can't see, when we don't even love someone we can see.

It's a point the theologians may have overlooked.

2. Praying

A conflict was threatening to tear apart the brand-new Jerusalem Church. Only a few days before, things had been going so smoothly—everybody working in harmony, new converts coming for instruction. Now the daily hand-outs to the more impoverished among the believers had exposed a major source of friction. Charges of racism were heard: it seems the Jewish Christians were being given larger portions than the Greeks.

According to the record, the twelve disciples quickly called the people together. The congregation was instructed to select a commission of seven Spirit-filled men to iron out the problem. As for themselves, the twelve had something else to do: "We will give ourselves steadfastly to the ministry of the Word and to prayer" (cf. Acts 6:4).

What kind of prayer do you suppose it was? Would they climb a mountain and hold an all-night vigil? Would they retire to hermit cells for private devotions? Would they organize prayer groups all over Judea and Samaria? My guess is that while they might have done these things, their chief intention was to do what they had seen Jesus do. Prayer, as Luther once said, is a social act. They would visit the homes of people and pray with them.

On January 9, 1972, as I knelt and felt hands laid on me and heard people interceding before God on my behalf, something happened to my whole approach to prayer. In the weeks that followed, I learned what a blessing comes to the one who does the praying.

Here's how it works: a few of us who have participated in "Afterglows" may be invited to a church, just as the disciples were invited into the homes of people. We hold a meeting, and those who wish prayer are asked to remain afterward. Someone expresses a special need and we take it to God. When all who want it have been prayed for, we go home.

For six years these prayer adventures have been going on, and I, for one, hope to continue them for the rest of my life. In those years I have prayed more than in all the rest of my years put together.

Three months after the January prayer meeting with the Thiessens, I traveled to Charlotte, North Carolina, to cover a Billy Graham crusade for *Decision* magazine. A school of evangelism was held concurrently with the meetings, and over a thousand pastors and their wives were in attendance.

One afternoon a team member telephoned me. "The school's main speaker for tomorrow morning is sick," he said. "You're to take his place."

"What's the subject?" I asked.

"The theology of evangelism. You will have one hour."

I rounded up a typewriter, Bible, and concordance, and spent the rest of the day in a scholastic frenzy. Next morning I took six single-spaced typewritten pages of notes into the pulpit and delivered a peroration that touched on every evangelistic reference in the Old and the New Testaments.

It was erudite, profound, and tedious.

Eventually I came to the end of the last page and looked at

my watch. Nearly thirty minutes of the hour remained. I closed the notebook and spent the rest of the time telling about the Canadian revival and what it had done for me.

After I finished a dozen ministers crowded around the pulpit. "We want an Afterglow," they said.

"When?"

"Tonight, here, after the meeting."

For the next two evenings we met in a circle, and I learned things about the ministry that were past all imagining. I also learned something about prayer.

When the disciples prayed with people it was nuts and bolts praying. They didn't waste time on painful silences, "unspoken requests," or timid smokescreen petitions that camouflaged the real need. Was there a problem? It was taken directly to the Lord.

A minister wrote inviting me to his church, expressing a desire to have his people "open up with their problems." As I explained to the minister, it is the Holy Spirit's business to pry, not ours. My function as a Christian brother is to convey love and talk to God about my friend who has asked for prayer about something. What my friend says, he says to God and not to me. That is the difference between the couch and the carpet.

One Wednesday evening I sat with eight or ten people in a pastor's study. The pastor had given us a list of sick folk to pray for while he delivered a lecture to 150 people in the sanctuary. After we had finished praying our way down the list, we still had half an hour until the lecture would be over. I suggested that we express our own needs and pray for each other. One person said she would like prayer for her father. Another mentioned a cousin half a continent away. I said, "Just this once let's not think about these other people. Let's pray instead for our own needs."

The lid came off. We learned that two of the people in that

group were afraid to go home, fearing what awaited them when they got there. An alert was sounded; angels of protection were summoned.

The disciples said, "We will give ourselves steadfastly to the ministry of the Word and to prayer."

In our time we seem to have given ourselves to just about everything else.

WHOSE FEET?

I love the fourth-century story of Hilarion the monk and Bishop Basil. Hilarion had a passion for solitude and had his heart set on going into the North African desert to live a hermit's life. Basil, bishop of Caesarea (who had also tried the solitary life) spoke to him about it. "Tell me," he said. "When you are out there by yourself, how can you be 'least of all'? And whose feet will you wash?"

Basil could also have reminded Hilarion of the biblical admonition to pray one for another, asking, "How will you work that in the desert?"

For millions of us churchgoers any kind of personal prayer is an awkward business, and to pray with another person is downright terrifying. That is why many of us prefer to let the person in the pulpit do the praying while we sit with heads bowed, lending the appearance of attention if not assent. I do not wish to impugn others, but while the minister is talking to God, my thoughts have often stolen off on business of their own.

"Our Father, we thank Thee for Thy manifold gifts to us" (I must pick up a valentine for my wife). . . . "and for the boundless measure of Thy love toward all mankind" (if he calls tomorrow we might wrap up that deal by the end of the week). . . . "We are grateful for the freedom we have to preach the Gospel" (why doesn't the preacher shave off that mustache?). . . . "and for the manifestations of Thy grace we have seen in the life of this church" (even if they are underdogs, the Vikings could take the Steelers if their quarterback would roll out more often). . . . "we pray for wisdom for our national leaders" (got to do something about that crabgrass) . . . "and we remember before Thee Alice Jurgensen in the hospital" (I believe this tooth is starting to kick up again) . . . "and we ask Thee to hear these petitions, together with the unspoken ones in our hearts, through Jesus Christ . . ."

Well, I say to myself, I got through it and no one was the wiser. I even remembered a few things I had to attend to. Who says prayer doesn't help?

Ole Hallesby, the Norwegian church leader, remarks that hell laughs and heaven weeps at such a farce.

But let's suppose a friend has come to us and asked us to pray for him. And let's suppose that instead of promising to do it at bedtime, we hunt a quiet spot together. Now what?

We ask what he wants prayer for, and then we pray. Not for what we think he needs, or for what the church says he needs, but for what he feels he needs. He may not tell us what those needs are because he is not sure we love him. He may put us off with some of his superficial needs. So we tell God how much we love this man. We write it in large letters across the scroll of heaven. We thank God for him and ask God to help him in Jesus' name.

All this praying is bathed in an atmosphere of thanksgiving as we praise God for what he is about to do in our friend's life. We claim the blessing before it happens just as Jesus taught us to do. What do you suppose will happen?

Don't be surprised if the brother starts to cry. He's not used to this kind of treatment in church. So we cry too.

Or perhaps the brother is just stunned. He was never up against God quite like this. We wait until the Holy Spirit suggests the next move.

Perhaps he will begin to level with God. It is an awesome thing to see a soul reach out its hand to its Creator—a step of pure faith, a venture into the unknown. Whatever happens, I doubt if he will ever forget the experience. Nor will you. Each time you meet thereafter, the memory of that prayer time will enrich your friendship.

If there was animosity, it will turn to love.

If there was defeat, it will turn to hope.

If there was doubt about God's Word, the Bible will suddenly become a beautiful book, because this is what the Bible is all about. Over and over it tells us that we learn to appropriate God's love through loving each other.

And as for prayer—instead of being an exercise in restlessness and inattention, it has become the fountainhead.

THE SPIRIT OF PRAYER

In a magnificent book that every Christian should read,* Ole Kristian Hallesby asks the question, "Why do most of us fail so miserably at prayer?"

I recall an evening meeting at Mount Hermon, California, years ago, when the Reverend Armin Gesswein asked if anyone present wished to be prayed for by others.

I raised my hand and said, "I am not a man of prayer. I would like to become one." Armin invited me to come to the front of the chapel and kneel. Several persons laid their hands on me and prayed for me.

It was the only time this happened in my nineteen years in the pastoral ministry. My devotional habits did not noticeably improve. I did not become a man of prayer, but I never forgot what the brethren did for me.

Today I am as slovenly as ever in my "quiet times," but I

---

* O. Hallesby, *Prayer*, tr. from Norwegian by C. J. Carlsen (Minneapolis: Augsburg, 1931).

have learned where the joy of prayer is to be found. I may neglect my own orisons until (I feel sure) the Lord has almost despaired of me, but I will cross two state lines to pray with someone else.

After an evening of seeing quiet miracles happen during prayer, I drive home asking myself, "What is keeping us from doing this all the time? Instead of taking sides against each other, singling out faults, condemning, and suing each other, why don't we just get on our knees and pray for each other? Didn't Arthur John Gossip, the Scottish preacher, say it is impossible to harbor ill will and animosity against others if you keep praying for them?"

Then I am forced to realize that I expect too much. As Paul says, until the love of God is poured out into our hearts by the Holy Spirit, we will continue to operate as human beings. To refer again to Hallesby, he says there is no use calling people to pray until the Spirit of Prayer is given; and the Spirit is not given until he is wanted. No demand, no supply.

Many churches are satisfied with themselves; they do not wish to be revived. Their club life is pleasant, the minister is a good fellow, he doesn't attack the Bible—why stir things up?

Revival demands a price in prayer. It demands a hunger and thirst after righteousness. "Everybody talkin' 'bout heaven ain't goin' there," and everybody talking about revival is not panting to be revived.

To give the appearance of revival a church will sometimes schedule a seminar on the subject, perhaps inviting a historian to lecture on great revivals of the past. I heard a man say during an Afterglow in Winnipeg, "I keep reading all these books on revival and the more I read, the colder I get." That happens. We can circle the flame for fifty years without getting singed.

While speaking at a Christian college in Florida, I gave an appeal to the students, suggesting that if any wished God to give them more love, they should come to the front of the meeting hall. Several did. While I was praying with them, about two hundred other students adjourned to a large room where chairs had been placed in a circle for an Afterglow.

The college president, a venerable, saintly brother, sat with the students and said, "Now, if anyone has anything to confess, this is a good time to do it. You're among friends."

I entered the room to find the circle sitting in frozen silence. *Confess? Friends?* I said, "With the president's permission I would like to offer a suggestion. Let's just go around the room and tell our names, and let those who would like prayer say so. Otherwise let them say, 'Praise the Lord,' and we'll pass along to the next."

The first young man on my right said he wanted prayer. Several students stepped into the center of the circle, knelt and prayed with him. The next person, a young woman, also asked for prayer. And the next.

Suddenly a young man out of turn left his seat and, walking across the room, he spoke to another student, and they went into a corner to pray. Some kind of breach was being healed. A young woman spoke to another student, and the same thing happened. Soon half a dozen prayer meetings were going on simultaneously. The room crackled with excitement. I did not know what to do.

A husky young man came up to me, tears streaming down his face. "If you stop this," he said, "God will never forgive you. We've been praying for three years for this to happen in our school."

The president had left, and we were half an hour past curfew. I looked to the elderly dean, and he said quietly, "Let it go on a while longer." The room was filled with cheering. Student after student then spoke his or her need and asked for prayer. It was an atmosphere of pure revival. But in the providence of God, within a short time a lull came and the meeting was dismissed with the singing of, "What a privilege to carry everything to God in prayer!"

Why do most of us fail so miserably at prayer? That's easy. We do it the wrong way.

INTERCESSORS

What is the holiest moment in an evangelistic meeting?

Is it when the massed choir reaches the high note of the anthem? When the evangelist goes into the invitation? When people in the audience move to the front under the prompting of the Spirit? Or when the inquirers are led in a prayer of commitment?

I don't think so. The holiest moment, to me, is when the volunteer counselor and the person who has come forward bow their heads and pray together.

Possibly the counselor lays his hand on the inquirer's shoulder, or takes him by the arm or hand. Why not? Elisha touched when he prayed. Our Lord Jesus Christ touched. Peter touched. John touched. Paul touched. Let's not talk about sensitivity training or touch therapy. Let's talk about New Testament ministry, about bearing each other's burdens. Paul calls it fulfilling the law of Christ. The Bible calls it intercession.

A curious passage in the prophecy of Isaiah (59:16) tells of God being displeased with his people, and ends with the words, "and he wondered that there was no intercessor."

No one to pray. No one to ask God to do something for somebody else.

In another passage, this one in Ezekiel (22:30), the Lord God declares, "I sought for a man ... that should make up the hedge and stand in the gap before me for the land, that I should not destroy it; but I found none."

What? All those priests moving about the altars in heavy

traffic, tending lamps, singing psalms, offering burnt sacrifices, collecting tithes, and there is not one intercessor available to stand before God on behalf of his people?

I wonder what God would say about our churches today.

A book on prayer lies before me. It is a fine book, dealing with the nature of prayer, methods of prayer, types of prayer, hindrances to prayer, and so on. It even has a chapter on answers to prayer. But it says nothing about Bob Selby, who lives across the street from a local church.

Bob's daughter was riding in a schoolbus when it jumped a guardrail and plunged down a 100-foot embankment. It happened over a year ago, and Bob still hasn't been able to put his life together.

If I understand the New Testament correctly, this man needs someone to pray for him and stand before God for him. Someone to love him.

He came to church one Sunday simply because he didn't know where else to turn. His wife thought it might help him. Bob didn't really want a sermon. He certainly didn't wish to join the church. He felt no need for any of the weekly meetings listed in the church bulletin. He couldn't have told you what he wanted.

The truth is, Bob Selby did not want to talk about his problem, but he did want someone who would talk to God for him about it. He wasn't fully aware of that fact, and, of course, the church didn't know it.

Bob required an intercessor. The church had its instructions and should have supplied one. "I urge," Paul wrote to Timothy, "that supplications, prayers, intercessions, and thanksgivings be made for all men. . . . This is good, and it is acceptable in the sight of God our Savior, who desires all men to be saved and to come to the knowledge of the truth" (2 Timothy 2:1, 3, 4, RSV).

Notice that Paul made prayer the basis of evangelism. This

was characteristic of the New Testament church, and the principle still works. When Christians intercede before God for others, God draws the others to himself. It is no secret that every great spiritual awakening in the history of the church was rooted and grounded in prayer. So when we pray for others we not only become intercessors we become evangelists. Someone prays with Bob Selby and Bob Selby is saved. The volunteer counselor talks to God about the inquirer at the evangelistic meeting and leads his new friend right into the Kingdom of Heaven.

That truly is the holiest moment.

STRAW MEN

"Confess your faults to one another"—so wrote the Apostle James in a letter addressed to the first-century churches (5:16).

But we don't. God pity us, we wouldn't think of it. "Good heavens! Who wants to listen to a recital of my weak points? I'd die before I'd blab my shortcomings to the church—or to anybody else (if they actually are shortcomings; from what I hear, I'm about as good as anybody in that church)."

If there is anything about revival that turns people off, it is the idea of confessing their sins. Baring intimate details during a church service, breast-beating, taking a psychological bath, unloading guilt feelings on the long-suffering congregation? Never!

So much for James and his first-century wisdom. "Put a lid on it! Cap it! Cool it! Damp it down! God is not the author of confusion, and the church is no place for vulgar displays."

I sympathize with people who talk that way, and share their distaste, but as far as I am concerned they are fighting a straw man. In six years of praying with Christian brothers and sisters, I have yet to hear anything that exceeded the canons of good taste. It seems the Holy Spirit has been monitoring the

Afterglows. I have heard people weep, I have heard them grapple candidly with their problems, but always the subject matter has been described in general terms. "I need more love for my family"; "I take people for granted"; "It's about a misunderstanding with my pastor"; "I'm too proud"; "Our daughter is away from the Lord; we can't communicate"— these are the requests we hear. So we pray.

And it was precisely this kind of confession I believe James had in mind; certainly not an artificial list of peccadilloes spewed from the pulpit and tailored for audience consumption.

One evening recently I spoke in a church on the West Coast. The pastor, an old friend, was, I knew, opposed to the kind of revival he had witnessed as a student in a Christian college. Nevertheless, when the time came, I extended an invitation to his people to come forward and ask God to fill their lives with his love.

As he saw the members of his church coming down front, some of them weeping, the pastor was deeply stirred. A few moments later, after I had led them in a prayer, I asked the pastor to close with the benediction. Instead he stepped into the pulpit and said, "I have been hurt. . . ."

He could speak no more; but a score of his parishioners who had come down front gathered about him on the platform and laid their hands on him. Three of his young people prayed for him.

He wrote me later, saying a dissident elder had greeted him affectionately after the service, and that he was "having a honeymoon with his congregation." I believe it.

What had the pastor "confessed"? Nothing—and every-thing. He divulged little, but he did speak of a problem of relationships in which he was involved. By bringing it to the surface he made visible his need, and the healing that the Apostle James said would take place, took place.

As long as we hide behind our opaque masks and set up

straw men to knock down, the church stays cold and ineffective. But when we become transparent, God begins to move. And that means we, too, must move.

When Christians finally begin to understand how important it is for them to clear away the obstacles that have deprived them of the Spirit-filled life, they set about making restitution. Such a move is not only commendable, it is absolutely essential. There is no revival without restitution.

But restitution can be dangerous.

I know a Christian woman who, under the prompting of the Spirit, as she believed, went to a sister in the church and told her, "For some time now I have held something against you, but the Lord has taken it away and I wanted you to know it."

She didn't need to say that. All God wanted her to do was to begin showing love to her sister. As it was, the sister was totally bewildered; she had no idea that any hostility existed between them. She decided to avoid the woman in the future lest she give her further cause for offense.

I don't say we should never confess a resentment held toward someone. Sometimes it may be vital if the air is to be cleared. But in every case the Spirit of God should be given perfect freedom to monitor the situation; and usually the less said, the better.

As Judy Sills of our Minneapolis Afterglow team said to a young man, "The Holy Spirit is always a gentleman."

MERCY FLIGHT

"I will pay Billy Graham a hundred dollars a minute if he will just listen to me!"

The speaker was an oilman wearing a large hat, sounding off in a hotel lobby in Houston, Texas. What was on his mind I'll never know, nor will Billy. But that night as I knelt by my bed in prayer I wondered, what does it take to get God to listen to us?

Unless someone is listening, our efforts to communicate are futile. Unless God hears, our prayers will bounce off the ceiling—and there will be no answers.

The Bible is the greatest manual on prayer ever written. It tells us again and again how we can make sure that our prayers are heard in the courts of heaven. Five points seem crucial:

1. We are to pray in the Name of Jesus.
2. We are to get rid of the iniquity in our hearts.
3. We are to face up to the fact of our spiritual pride.
4. We are to be filled with the Holy Spirit.
5. We are to love our neighbor.

These five points are simply different ways of saying that we need an infilling of the love of God if our prayers are to get anywhere. The Letter of James says that the "effectual fervent prayer" of a righteous person "availeth much" (5:16). The Greek word for "effectual fervent" is *energoumene,* which actually means "set in operation." And if I read my Bible correctly, operative praying is praying in love.

Let me illustrate: Certain well-known Christian organizations are shipping food and medicine as disaster relief to different parts of the globe. Winola and I know these people, and when they write asking for help in sending sacks of grain and rice and pharmaceuticals to stricken populations, we respond.

We know that the emergency supplies carried on mercy flights will not solve the basic problems of the area. Housing, self-supporting industries, dam construction—all these will be needed to create a viable economy.

What the food and medicine do is meet an immediate, desperate condition right now. And that is what love does when we pray for someone. Love is the mercy flight that God

dispatches to the lonely and forlorn heart. Love is the parame-
dic who brings first aid to the victim. Love won't pay the rent,
it won't cut out the tumor, but it will provide mouth-to-mouth
resuscitation for the soul.

There's little point in digging wells or building dams in a
developing country if everyone has died of starvation; and
there's little hope for the person who needs prayer if the love
is absent. Love suffuses everything about human relationships
in a kind of heavenly beauty, no matter how bad things are.

Once God pours in the love, we are operating in a different
atmosphere. The love is God's assurance that he will do something about our situation. He will not ignore it or allow it to
deteriorate beyond what we can bear. In some way he will
intervene for good.

When we pray in love, the one we pray for will be better
for it. If he feels our love, we can be sure the Spirit of God is at
work.

Is our friend outside of Christ? God will show us how we
can help him.

Is our friend a discouraged believer? Look for a change.

On the other hand, when we somehow fail to pray in love,
God's reaction may be negative. To the religious people of
ancient Israel who had refused to treat their neighbors loving-
ly, he said:

> I hate, I despise your feasts, and I take no delight in your solemn
> assemblies. Even though you offer me your burnt offerings and
> cereal offerings, I will not accept them, . . . What to me is the
> multitude of your sacrifices? . . . When you spread forth your
> hands, I will hide my eyes from you; even though you make many
> prayers, I will not listen . . . (Amos 5:21-22, Isa. 1:11, 15, RSV).

But first aid is after all first aid. Just because Christians
begin showing love to each other and praying for each other, it
doesn't mean that the revival is on. Sacks of rice are not houses

and dams. Wrongs in the church must be set right, restitutions made, differences reconciled, abuses removed. But prayer will certainly help; and when people feel loved, Jesus Christ is glorified. As the Apostle John said, we know we have passed from death to life because we love the brothers and sisters.

When a church is baptized in love—as at Pentecost—it really doesn't need revival, for God has heard and responded. The Holy Spirit has already moved in.

3. Crucifying

"Any 'Christian' experience," I remember Pastor McLeod saying in Winnipeg, "that does not begin at the cross of Jesus Christ is suspect." So we must go back to the ancient records for the roots of what we have said so far.

A not-so-green hill may be seen rising just outside the ancient Damascus gate to Jerusalem. On that hill many years ago, by the Gospel accounts, a detail of Roman soldiers planted three crosses, two of which served as gallows for convicted robbers.

On the third cross Jesus of Nazareth, the Prince of Glory, the Savior of the world, was crucified. He shed his blood there not just for the satisfaction of divine justice, not just to overcome evil, not just for the church, or even for the human race, but for me. Me and my sins.

Jesus Christ died on my behalf and in my stead, that I might stand justified and guiltless before God, a forgiven sinner. It was an act of authentic, pristine love, and it saved me forever from the powers of Satan and darkness.

The day I believed that truth and accepted it for myself was the day I became a Christian. God in his wisdom has not allowed me to know which day that was, but it occurred in 1941 and was the greatest event of my life.

Thirty years later I went to Canada and learned about a fourth cross. I guess I had known about it all along. The first Bible verse that Winola ever quoted to me, during our courting days back in 1940, was Galatians 2:20, "I am crucified with Christ . . ." And I was familiar with Thomas Shepherd's lines in the hymn "Maitland,"

... there's a cross for ev'ry one,
And there's a cross for me.

But the Canadians took me beyond individual texts and Gospel tunes and showed me that the fourth cross was to be found throughout the New Testament; furthermore, it was for me. If I wished to be rid of the disappointment and dissatisfaction that were plaguing my life, if I wished to be filled with the Spirit, I would have to die to self.

Die to self! The words used to roll so easily off my lips. I had been using them for years without really mortifying the flesh or experiencing the crucified life.

Now I was told that there was no way I could set out in quest of this life, no sudden resolution or rededication, no shaving of the head or taking a vow, no search for some fleeting holy grail that would help me. I would simply have to reckon myself dead, as the Apostle Paul says, in a faith commitment (Rom. 6:11).

I learned that it's not enough to talk about coming to the cross, being near the cross, yielding ourselves at the cross, laying our burdens at the foot of the cross, taking up the cross, or bearing the cross. Crucifixion means we have to be nailed to the cross. And since self cannot and will not slay self, it has to be done by faith. We consider it done; we reckon ourselves dead by faith.

The cross means the end of the trail. It is the final collapse of pride. The house of cards so carefully built up by fingertip skill and effort comes tumbling down. Everything the ego has tried to do for itself grinds to a dead halt: fame, glory, niche in history, pride of accomplishment, track record, even sanctimony and sense of personal worth.

I learned too that the Holy Spirit loves a vacuum. When he sees a soul emptied of self, contrite and open, he will come in providing he is invited. As the evangelist Sam P. Jones once put it, the Lord fishes on the bottom.

Since I have referred to Bill McLeod's teaching, let me add what he once wrote for me on the subject of crucifixion, in an article published in *Decision* magazine:*

> For many years I searched for victory over sin and for spiritual power. I knew that the two were related but did not know in what way. I read every book I could lay my hands on, dealing with the Holy Spirit, revival and related themes. I spent hours praying for the power of the Holy Spirit. At times I tried praying through whole nights, hoping to overcome what I felt to be God's disinclination. I had not learned the truth so well expressed by Archbishop Richard Trench: "Prayer is not overcoming God's reluctance; it is laying hold of his highest willingness."
>
> The time finally came when God brought me to the complete end of self-effort and striving. I died to self and sin. The moment this happened I experienced a filling of the Holy Spirit without even asking for it.
>
> Four weeks later, on October 13, 1971, a great revival broke in my church in Saskatoon.*

THE SKULL

In his novel *Heaven's My Destination*, Thornton Wilder describes a man traveling through the South on a train and

---

* "Getting at the Root," *Decision*, Vol. 16, 6 (June 1974), p. 4. © 1974 by the Billy Graham Evangelistic Association. Reprinted by permission.

being approached by an earnest young man who wishes to speak with him about "the most important thing in life." The older man stretches out his legs and drawls, "Son, if it's insurance, I got too much, if it's oil wells, I don't touch 'em, and if it's religion, I'm saved."

When I first heard from my Canadian friends that I needed to be crucified with Christ, I reacted somewhat in the same way. Using Winola's verse (Gal. 2:20), I pointed out that the Bible says I am already crucified with Christ as a Christian believer, so there is really nothing more I can do about it.

Theologically I had some footing, since when the Apostle Paul (whom I was quoting) said he hung on the cross with Christ, he was in a sense speaking for all of us in the faith. But it is one thing to be theologically correct and another to have one's hide nailed to a piece of wood at Calvary. My mind was with Paul but my body was A.W.O.L.

When God brought me to my knees late one night in January, 1972, it was explained to me by Harry and Evelyn Thiessen that Jesus declared himself willing to go to the cross in obedience to his Father, and we must be equally willing. And since our going to the cross involves a radical break with our former behavior—whether it happens at conversion or later—it has to be God's work, not ours. Our own attempts to stop sinning and quit our meanness are about as successful as a democracy's effort to create morality by enacting legislation. Only the Holy Spirit can neutralize and render powerless the forces of evil.

What are *we* expected to do? To begin with, let's think about that word *Calvary*, found in the older English translations in Luke 23:33. It comes from the Latin word *calvaria*, which is a translation of the Greek word *kranion*, which is in turn a translation of the Aramaic word *Golgotha*, meaning *skull*. The place where Jesus was put to death was called The Place of the Skull. Like the valley of Hinnom (Gehenna) on the other side of Jerusalem, it quite possibly was a site for the burning of refuse, including the corpses of animals and criminals.

With Calvary in mind, let's review some of the personal acquisitions we have become accustomed to thinking of as necessities, essential to our station in life. Fine clothes, automobiles, campers, boats, cottages at the shore, expensive hobbies and habits, sportive indulgences, pets, libraries—are we ready to give them up?

Next, let us look at the treasures, souvenirs, and mementoes that have meant so much to us as tokens of achievement and recognition—our honors, trophies, badges, medals, citations, awards of merit, diplomas, testimonials, certificates, titles, clippings, plaques: Are we ready to cart these, such as they are, out to The Place of the Skull?

Then let us inventory our properties, investments, bank accounts, equities, retirement funds, and personal effects. We may protest that such accumulation is hardly suitable for the refuse heap. After all, the Bible tells us to be good stewards.

Ah, yes. But now we are speaking of Calvary, and stewardship is not the issue. Crucifixion is not being a good steward, crucifixion is the steward turning back the property to his Master.

And so we come to the position we have attained in life or hope to attain. All our days we have struggled for it—our rank, class, status, reputation, the esteem in which we are held in our group, the rung we have reached on the ladder. Jesus made himself of no reputation for our sakes and chose the way of the cross. If we would follow him, it means everything respecting our position in life has to be willingly set out on the sidewalk; the sanitation department will be around to pick it up.

Must we also give up our friends, our associates, our loved ones who don't understand what has happened to us? By no means. Scripture contains no specific order for us to abandon those we love. Jesus did not. Our friends may abandon us (as his did), but the Spirit has called us to love them whether or not they leave us.

Someone asked Dr. Will Houghton, one-time president of Moody Bible Institute, how much a certain person left in his estate at his death, and Dr. Houghton replied, "He left it all." That is what happens at The Place of the Skull. When we are reduced to what they left our Lord, we are ready to go on.

THE WHITE STONE

I grew up with a dismal self-image. I came across to myself as repulsive, of no account and badly put together, and I had reasons for believing that others agreed with me. During my high school years no prizes or trophies decorated my room. Recognition came seldom, and seemed accidental. It seemed highly unlikely to me that I would succeed at anything.

I even disliked being a clergyman's son. To my young eyes our family was unlike other families, being dependent upon "charity," that is, on whatever people put in the offering plate.

As I recall, things bottomed out for me during a college glee club tour of Europe when I was nineteen years old. At a swimming pool in Dresden, Germany, one of my colleagues looked me over and remarked, "Wirt, you've got pimples all over your back."

It seems such a trivial and incongruous thing, but added to all my other woes leading to self-rejection, it was the end. I became inconsolable; life appeared utterly bleak.

So today when the importance of a good self-image is increasingly stressed in psychological theory, I will testify to the need for that stress.

After struggling to survive in the Depression years, I found my self-confidence gradually beginning to rise. Unfortunately there ballooned with it a cockiness that affected my social relationships and made me ambitious out of all proportion to my abilities. And therein lies a dilemma.

It is well known that a person's low self-esteem can have disastrous results. The relationship between a low concept of self and antisocial or criminal behavior has been established beyond question. Among Christian educators today the concept of self-worth, self-esteem, self-acceptance, seems in some cases almost as vital as a sound theology.

How then do we reconcile self-acceptance with what we have been considering: self-crucifixion? How does the need for a healthy estimate of the self relate to the New Testament's antagonism toward self-centeredness, and its demand that the self be "put to death" (Col. 3:5, RSV) in order that Jesus Christ might take over the personality?

In my own case the wretched opinion I once held of my person was outgrown, but woe is me! My expanding self-image began to flourish like a green bay tree. Pride of self, unleashed and without Christian curb or restraint, outstripped itself. The Dr. Jekyll of self-acceptance became the Mr. Hyde of self-worship.

Today I can identify with the identity crises of many outside Christ, and can understand why they are asking, "Who am I?" "What am I for?" "How can I achieve a proper self-image?"

Often these questionings seem to echo the spirit of Nora Helmer, the heroine of Ibsen's play *A Doll's House*, written just a century ago. In the final scene Nora informs her husband that she no longer loves him and is leaving home. When her husband reproaches her by saying, "First and foremost, you are a wife and mother," Nora replies, "I believe that first and foremost I am an individual, just as much as you are—or at least I'm going to try to be. . . . I have to think things out for myself and get things clear."

Something in us may respond positively to Nora's "emancipation proclamation." The problem is not her desire for self-identity, the problem is her loss of love. When love flies out the window, something else creeps in. The theologians call it pride, vanity, *hubris*, arrogance, loftiness, self-love. The Bible calls it sin.

Psychologists are right in desiring to implant a sense of true worth and self-appreciation (a better word than self-love) in every child. But what a quick step it is from those well-known feelings of inadequacy and inferiority to a colossal egoism that feeds on snobbishness and takes a deadly toll in human relations.

The New Testament is vividly aware of this danger. The Apostle Paul writes to church leaders in Rome and Galatia:

> Don't cherish exaggerated ideas of yourself or your importance, but try to have a sane estimate of your capabilities by the light of the faith that God has given to you all. (Rom. 12:3).
> If a man thinks he is "somebody," he is deceiving himself, for that very thought proves that he is nobody (Gal. 6:3, Phillips)

From a psychological point of view such words may sound terrifying to those seeking self-identity. Perhaps they already think of themselves as "nobody"; now the Bible confirms it!

But Paul is not writing to victims of the computer age who are struggling with self-awareness. He is writing to Christians who are practicing one-upmanship on their fellow Christians instead of loving them. He is telling them that they need to give up their stiff-necked behavior and be nailed to the cross.

Recently I discussed the self-image question with Ralph Sutera, one of the evangelistic leaders whom God used in the Canadian revival. His comment was, "Crucifixion does not mean that the self is dead, but that we are dead to self. It does not bring death to the personality, but rather to those things that bring contamination and destruction to the personality."

When I suggested the need we have for a good self-image, he said, "There can be only one self-image for a Christian, and that is the image of God. Christ is the one sure source of our self-esteem."

"But if it's of Christ, then it's not of self," I pointed out.

"Exactly," he said.

And that must be where we leave the matter. It is a paradox.

When the Holy Spirit comes and dwells in the life of the believer, God imparts to his child a sense of divine significance, of holy purpose, beyond any stretch of the human imagination. "I can do all things in him who strengthens me" (Phil. 4:13).

But first the Spirit must have full sovereignty! He will liberate us from the demands and contrivings of the self and give us Life with a capital L, but only if he is given control. He brooks no competition.

Professor Thomas Howard of Amherst College (in an article in *Christianity Today**) has suggested that the matter of the believer's identity—that is, of self-worth, coming to terms with oneself—may never fully be known because it is God's secret. He quotes the passage in Revelation, "To him that overcometh will I give a white stone, and in the stone a new name written, which no man knoweth saving he that receiveth it" (Rev. 2:17).

Professor Howard comments, "Your identity, perhaps, is a treasure, precious beyond your wildest imaginings, kept for you by the great Custodian of souls to be given to you at the Last Day when all things are made whole."

But as I read that passage of Scripture I note that the treasure is *already ours;* we know the secret name on the white stone. Perhaps no one else does, but we do.

And that to me is identity enough.

---

* "Who am I? Who am I?" *Christianity Today*, v. xxi (July 8, 1977), pp. 10-13.

DISALLOWANCE

For a while let us leave Jerusalem and The Place of the Skull and journey northward into lovely Galilee with its quiet blue lake and rolling hillsides, and its sheep grazing by the water's edge.

Jesus has taken his disciples away from the crowd to a hill known today as the Mount of Beatitudes. He has seated himself and has opened his mouth. Let's join the others and listen. His first words are, "Blessed are the poor in spirit, for theirs is the Kingdom of Heaven" (Matt. 5:3).

We back away. What kind of talk is that? *Poor in spirit?* We cannot have heard aright. Does he really mean that the spiritually weak, the spiritually barren, are blessed? How extraordinary! Coming from the Head of the Church, such a statement, if taken seriously, could send shock waves through the entire evangelical community.

It almost seems as if Jesus should offer a retraction for making such a statement. It contradicts, apparently, everything our Bible-believing churches are attempting to instill into their people Sunday after Sunday.

What can Jesus mean? If God blesses the poor in spirit, what becomes of that vital spiritual life everyone keeps talking about? Is Jesus suggesting that our churches become like "the other kind," who burble through their ecclesiastical routine and let it go at that?

No.

Jesus is saying simply that we must be emptied of spirit before we can be filled with the Holy Spirit. The spirits of this world, including the "religious" spirits, have to go because they are all human-based, human-contrived, human-promoted, human-controlled and human-serving. They are vehicles of the most damning possession of all, spiritual pride.

Crucifixion of the self will never be complete until this

problem has been faced, dealt with, and solved. The Holy Spirit does not wish to hurt our pride, he wants to kill it. That is the verdict of the New Testament Gospels and Epistles.

Spiritual pride was the problem of ancient Israel:

> Who shall ascend into the hill of the Lord? Or who shall stand in his holy place? He that hath not lifted up his soul unto vanity. (Ps. 24:34)

It was the problem of the religious leaders of Jesus' day:

> When you pray, you must not be like the hypocrites; for they love to stand and pray in the synagogues and at the street corners, that they may be seen by man. (Matt. 6:5, RSV)

It was the problem of the early church:

> I have written something to the church; but Diotrephes, who likes to put himself first, does not acknowledge my authority. . . . He refuses to welcome the brethren, and also stops those who want to welcome them, and puts them out of the church. (3 John 9-10, RSV)

And it is still our problem. "Personal vanity," says John R. W. Stott, the English evangelical leader, "lies at the root of most dissensions in every local church today."

When we tell our friends that we have been "really growing spiritually this past year," we may mean it sincerely but such language is a snare. What are we saying? That we are proud of ourselves for going to Bible class?

Think of Jesus on the cross with his cry of dereliction, "My God, my God, why hast thou forsaken me?"

Today it is not Sherwood Wirt the evildoer who grieves the Holy Spirit so much as Sherwood Wirt the proud Christian, who is tempted to think he has arrived at a higher spiritual level than someone else. You see, I read two chapters of my Bible daily; my neighbor reads only one. I have concluded that

I must be "moving out spiritually," while he—well, of course, I'm not to judge, but he seems to be barely treading water. Incidentally I have completely forgotten to love the guy.

God brands my thinking "vanity of vanities."

If "blessed are the poor in spirit" means anything at all, it means that all of my claims to spiritual achievement are disallowed, and I am left at the cross. Self-sufficiency, complacency, pride of life, condescension, class consciousness, church standing—these are the final items on the inventory to be discarded at The Place of the Skull.

Crucifixion is not a way of self-realization but of self-sacrifice. It is the way not to spiritual riches but to spiritual poverty, not to spiritual growth but to spiritual shrinkage. It turns out not spiritual giants but spiritual pygmies.

It is only when we let go of the rope that we discover that underneath are the everlasting arms. It is only when we have no spirit left at all that we receive the filling of the Holy Spirit.

HEEP AND CŒCUS

"Have you heard my sermon on humility?" my friend the late Reverend George Edstrom used to ask, adding, "It's the greatest sermon I ever preached."

As a non-Christian and later as a Christian I spent most of my life bouncing back and forth between humility and pride without knowing how to handle either one. If I crowed about something I'd done, the Lord sent me a guilty twinge. I'd laugh lamely and say (quoting some unknown early Englishman), "He that tooteth not his own horn, the same shall not be tooted." If recognition was bestowed upon me for some act, I pretended to put on a modest demeanor, but inwardly I was pleased as punch and wondered why it hadn't come sooner. If I managed to do something in a rare and humble spirit, the performance yielded so much personal satisfaction that my ego could hardly restrain itself.

So I zigzagged between Dickens' Uriah Heep and William Law's Cœcus, between the hypocrite who hides his self-conceit behind a mask of meekness and servility, and the imperious swaggerer whose professed love for modest persons blinds him to his own insufferable arrogance.*

It's fair to ask whether after I became a Christian I really did want to be humble. Certainly I wanted to obey Scripture, and Scripture is clear on the matter: "Walk humbly . . ." (Mic. 6:8); "be clothed with humility . . ." (1 Peter 5:5); "put on humbleness of mind . . ." (Col. 3:12); "blessed are the meek . . ." (Matt. 5:5); "in lowliness of mind let each esteem others better than themselves . . ." (Phil. 2:3); "God resists the proud but gives grace to the humble . . ." (James 4:6).

But did I want to be humble? I wanted people to think I was humble. And I had no desire to be a prig. For seventeen years I worked for the evangelist Billy Graham and learned the man's secret: it was a genuine humility. I coveted that. The trouble was, I was as proud as a peacock to be on his team.

Many people have given up altogether the idea of being humble. They say it is a put-on and a waste and has no place in the modern world. They're accomplished and brilliant, they know it, and they're not afraid to say so. "Why fight it?" they ask. Such people may be publicly admired and even envied for their forthrightness, but I notice they are seldom liked.

It's the modest, unassuming, quiet person who is more apt to capture the affection of the public. The Psalmist once wrote that God does not despise a humble heart, and in that respect, at least, most people are like their Maker.

Patrick, the patron saint of Ireland, was a humble man, although one might not gain that impression watching the

---

*Cf. Law, A Serious Call to a Devout and Holy Life (1728), ch. 16.

ostentatious parades around the world on St. Patrick's Day, or visiting the ornate cathedrals named for him. But in his *Confession*, one of the two early documents correctly attributed to him, Patrick identifies himself in these words: "I, Patrick, a sinner, the most awkward of country bumpkins, the least of all the faithful, and the most contemptible among very many."

Augustine, probably the greatest theologian the church has produced, was a humble person. In his youth he was exorbitantly ambitious and was determined to become one of the most important persons in the Roman Empire, a "friend of the emperor." Then he was converted. In his *Confessions*, he tells us what swayed him: It was not the church, it was not even the Bible; it was the Person of the meek and lowly Jesus. To Augustine the Psalms became "hymns of faith and devotion that break the pompous spirit."

So how did I become humble?

Did I crawl on my hands and knees ten miles to church? Had I done so, you can be sure I would have boasted about it. Did I wash someone's feet? No, because today we wear shoes. Humiliation, it seems, is not necessarily the road to humility.

Did I "let it all hang out" by writing for publication a diary of contrition and soul-baring? No publisher I know would want such drivel from me, and if he did release it I would probably be sued.

Please understand that the issue of my humility did not involve my relationship to God. That was settled for eternity when I came to Christ. I felt and still feel totally humbled before Deity. To walk under the canopy of the stars, to read a psalm at bedtime, is to enter a world in which I am submissive and at peace.

My problem has always been with people; I was not willing to prefer others ahead of me, to esteem someone better than myself, or to put myself last. I knew that Jesus had told us to take the seats at the foot of the banqueting table. I knew that the whole meaning of the incarnation was that God became a human being and humbled himself even to the cross. But I wasn't ready to eat humble pie when it was served up by people I thought were beneath me.

So how did I become humble? I didn't. I just stopped thinking about it. I went back to square one and asked the Lord to crucify me.

Every morning the devil talks to me about my humility. He tells me that I am making great spiritual progress and growing into a very humble person; but the devil is a liar. By the grace of God I am finished with pretense and posturing and pseudo-modesty; through with worrying about whether I am conveying a proper impression of reticence.

Once we are filled with the Spirit and with love, our minds are turned to other things and the subject of self becomes irrelevant. The Christian simply loses his identity in the needs, interests, and aspirations of others.

That's where the joy is.

JESUS

Our expedition into Galilee has ended; we have returned to The Place of the Skull. On this hill of death we put life in perspective and assess its values.

Progress, the car that I thrilled to ride in as a growing boy, picked up a burst of speed in the twentieth century, then fishtailed into a roadblock. Its passengers were thrown out and landed in a patch of weeds.

Among the facts to be considered are:
The second law of thermodynamics.
The future of democracy.
The eroding of natural resources.
The international arms buildup.

The pollution of the planet.

The shredding of the moral fabric.

The hostility of races and peoples toward each other.

The condition of the church.

One added fact remains to be considered: my own condition.

My Christian life began, like creation itself, under the superintendence of the Holy Spirit. It was the Spirit who first drew me to Jesus Christ and sealed me with the promise of eternal life. Whatever it was that happened, he did it.

But now time has elapsed. Life has been hard; an attrition has set in; the wear and tear of human relationships has brought about in me a kind of spiritual arteriosclerosis. I don't find it easy to be sweet any more. The old urge and desire for prayer, for Bible study, for witnessing has subsided into lethargy. I've picked up some rather long-standing grudges.

It isn't that I have degenerated into a backsliding, dissolute sinner. It's just that something I used to have has been mislaid somewhere, and I'm no longer a very nice person to be around. I've become oversensitive to my own hurts and insensitive to others'.

That is why I—and Christians who are like me—must return to The Place of the Skull. It is precisely at this place that we are to take stock of ourselves.

There are no churches here.

No synagogues.

No clergy.

No religious orders.

No choirs.

No litanies.

No church notices in the newspapers.

No Easter sunrise TV happenings by satellite.

No youth camps.

No religious conventions.

No Gospel music or film festivals.

No international parachurch organizations.

No appeals for funds.

No shepherds or wise men.

No Pharisees or Sadducees.

No false human spirits.

No demonic spirits—Paul declared they have all been exposed and triumphed over in this place.

No people claiming to be privy to some arcane knowledge about the Holy Spirit on which to preen themselves or build an aura of spirituality.

Just Jesus.

But from our cross we look through the darkness to his cross and we murmur to him, "Remember me when You come in Your kingly power."

And in that place of death and devastation he sees us as we are, stripped and emptied of everything, even of spirit; and he says to us what he said to one long ago, "Truly I say to you, today you shall be with me in Paradise" (Luke 23:43).

And that's enough. When we reach the nadir in our personal lives where we can say, "Lord, put me on the cross," that very day Jesus says, "You shall be with me."

We are content; we ask no more.

But now we find that we are not alone after all; many others have joined us. Not only the penitent thief who was crucified with Jesus, but other desperate people are to be seen:

Abraham is there, not knowing which way to go. Moses is there with a price on his head. David is there feeling like a pelican of the wilderness or an owl of the desert; and all his bankrupt, distressed, and discontented cave dwellers are with him. Hezekiah is there mourning, as he says, like a dove, and chattering like a swallow. The starving widow of Zarephath is there with her last handful of meal. Mary the lowly hand-maiden of the Lord is there, and Mary Magdalene, weeping. And Peter the denier and Paul the chief of sinners are there.

And all the poor in spirit, from that day to this, of every race and continent, who in their despondency and despair have looked to Jesus. All at the cross, and the hounds are skulking nearer, and the carrion birds are beginning to circle.

It is God's move.

4. Waiting

January in Minnesota is a season that seems to be enjoyed mostly by crows, snowmobile racers, and wall-eyed pike. Anyone with sense stays home. On the particular Sunday evening in January 1972 when I prayed to be filled with the Holy Spirit, some two dozen not-too-sensible people were there with me in the basement of that Minneapolis church. A number of them prayed and asked God to be filled as I did. There being no further business, the meeting adjourned.

Next day Harry and Evelyn Thiessen were on their way back to Canada, and I was at my typewriter as usual, polishing a piece for the Easter issue of *Decision* magazine and working up advance material about the coming Billy Graham crusades in Charlotte, North Carolina, and Cleveland, Ohio.

Evenings were devoted to finishing a book manuscript, while Winola watched television downstairs, alone.

About midweek I became vaguely aware that something pleasant, and therefore different, was happening inside me. I wasn't prepared to tie it to any specific event—certainly not to the previous Sunday evening—but when I visited with some friends who had been at that meeting I learned that something had happened to them also.

A warm feeling spread through me, making me want to lift my voice in praise of the name of Jesus all the time. Much to my surprise, I no longer held any bitterness toward anyone. As I said earlier, my home situation improved; I simply came downstairs.

Daily depressions that had afflicted me for years, making me want to drop suddenly in my tracks and say, "I give up," disappeared. No longer did those negative feelings come and go; they went. The world around me, even North Vietnam, seemed no longer my battlefield, but rather a part of life to be loved.

The thing I wished most to do was pray with people. Goal-setting, ambition, promotion, had all been called in for retooling. My thinking was routed into a new channel. In spite of myself I kept smiling and felt silly doing it, but love and happiness had filled my cup, and I couldn't help it or do a thing about it.

Such marks of God's freshness were not unfamiliar to me from my reading. I knew what to expect, even if I didn't expect it. During thirty years in the ministry, no showers of blessing had fallen, but there had been occasional mercy-drops. I served four parishes, did a stint in the student ministry, went overseas as a military chaplain, and put in twelve years as Billy Graham's editor. God's faithful care was often evident.

For a long time the subject of revivalism had fascinated me, even though I had ho-hummed the first reports of revival that came in from western Canada. I had combed many volumes on the subject, had visited so-called revival meetings, and had even written and edited a volume entitled *Spiritual Awakening*.

Yet despite my struggles to be revived, and my eagerness to become a prayed-up, victorious, God-honoring, witnessing, soul-winning Christian, I had not arrived there. And now it appeared that I had been filled with the Holy Spirit with no effort, without even being aware of it.

As I look back on that week, the explanation lies in one word: waiting.

The book of Acts makes it clear that God does not necessarily produce on order. He is not Room Service. We do not walk to the front of the church and zap! we are saved.

God is God. He is not wired to human controls. He is omnipotent, immortal, immutable, all-wise, all-knowing, the Sovereign Majesty, the Creator of the heavens and the earth. He moves at his own good pleasure and he demands that we wait.

Jesus sent the disciples back to Jerusalem to wait for the promise of the Father. Some days later the Spirit came at Pentecost. I too had to wait, and didn't even know I was waiting. Evidently that's the way God wanted it.

One night I asked the Holy Spirit to fill me, and next day I was back on the job. Perhaps I should have been keen with expectation, full of good "vibes," but I wasn't. No doubt I had browsed too much in the field and was overfamiliar with the "varieties of religious experience."

Because God is a God of variety, not everyone has to wait. For some of us it is a discipline. God wants us to take our hands off the matter and turn our request over to him. During our waiting time, we are not even to pray about the Holy Spirit. As I read my New Testament, it was not prayer that ushered in Pentecost. We are not told that people prayed, just that they were together in one place.

It is my conviction that praying up a storm and battering the gates of heaven will not bring the filling of the Spirit. We ask; then we wait. The time lag is important because God can then exercise his Crown rights. He has freedom in which to move. We are past the point of tearful firm resolves, deep commitments, vigils upon our knees. Noble intentions based upon a lifetime of listening to Christian exhortation do not count here.

When I enrolled as a doctoral candidate at Edinburgh University, I was at pains to bring with me all the grades and records from postgraduate courses I had taken at American seminaries. When I tried to find some Scottish worthy to give them to, I was informed in mild tones, "You won't be needing those here. Unless you so wish, you won't even be expected to attend classes. Your work will be judged by your thesis."

It's my feeling that before he ascended into heaven, Jesus may have said to his disciples something like this: "You won't need any credits now. You can put away the hours you have tagged after me, and all your efforts to spruce up your behavior and make yourself worthy of me. You can forget your victories and failures. Whether you achieved, underachieved, or over-achieved doesn't matter. What you need now is love for each other. Go back to Jerusalem and wait."

Charles Williams, the English author, once wrote, "Usually the way must be made for heaven, and then it will come by some other; the sacrifice must be made ready, and the fire will strike on another altar." * It's like saying (if I may make the analogy) that when you drop a coin in the slot of one vending machine, the product may come out of another. That's because God is free. His ways are not our ways. He moves according to the sublimity of his own desire. He hears our prayer that we might be Spirit-filled, but when he sends his Spirit, it is not at the time or in the way we expected.

I put my money in the slot, and it was a Canadian coin. It shouldn't have worked, but it did, later, in another machine. I

---

* Charles Williams, *He Came Down from Heaven* (London: Heinemann, 1938), p. 25.

had asked God to make some changes in other people. Instead he changed me.

THE LAST COMMAND

"Wait in the city of Jerusalem until you are clothed with power from on high."

Except for his benediction, those were the final words his disciples would hear from the lips of Jesus on the Mount of Olives before he was lifted from their sight according to Luke 24:49.

"Wait." That's what the Man said. "Don't leave town. Wait." Some of the most moving passages in the Bible—and in all literature—make a similar point:

"Rest in the Lord, and wait patiently for him: fret not thyself. . . ."

"I wait for the Lord, my soul doth wait, and in his word do I hope."

Unfortunately I don't like to wait, and many other Christians share my feeling. "My schedule calls for close connections; I can't afford to wait. The King's business demands haste. If I am to meet my goals and commitments, a wait is unthinkable. The world will go to hell while I wait."

And yet there it stands in Scripture: Jesus commanded "that they should not depart from Jerusalem, but wait." The most important movement in the history of the world was about to be launched, and their orders were to wait.

It's worth pondering how much of the agony in our churches may have its origin right here. Could it be said that Jesus is also telling us also to wait? And if he is, in view of the tensions and pressures of modern living, is it really possible for a Christian to wait upon God?

I think many of us would rather do anything than wait.

When we drive to the airport to meet an incoming plane and it is late, we don't know what to do with ourselves.

So I have a suggestion for my fellow Christians. (Suggestions are rare with me now.) Once we have invited the Lord to crucify us, to remove the obstructions that have kept our lives from being Spirit-filled, let our waiting be a time of quiet inner refreshing as we go about what we do. Let's be expectant, but not too expectant.

Don't imagine for a moment that the disciples spent ten days in a Jerusalem upper room doing absolutely nothing. They went home; they changed clothes; they washed; they slept; they ate; they worked at their duties; they loved their families. And so should we. The point of waiting is not that we should become inert, but that we should give God's love full sway in our lives. Much Christian effort has been damaged by the rash haste of the planners. To blow our own work is bad enough, but to blow a work for God is tragic.

WHAT ARE WE WAITING FOR?

Much of my early life was spent waiting for things that providentially never happened.

I waited for a movie scout to discover me; for a chance to become the school hero; for a lucky drawing; for the boss' daughter to fall in love with me; for an editor to accept my manuscript.

After I became a Christian it didn't take long to recognize the worldliness of such "great expectations." Instead I began looking forward to our Lord's return.

Some years later, when I was deeply involved in Christian activities, it occurred to me that I was not waiting for the Lord as much as I formerly had done. Instead I was spending much time waiting for a committee to act, waiting for an invitation to arrive, and, above all, waiting for a proper recognition of my gifts and efforts on the part of those to whom I was responsible.

I had to admit that things hadn't changed much.

I saw my friends doing the same things, and I wondered whether the history of the world could not be written as a wait:

Think of nations waiting for their rulers to die.

Oppressed peoples waiting for a deliverer who will lift the yoke of the tyrant.

Tribes around the Mediterranean shore waiting for a Messiah to come (but when he appeared he was virtually unrecognized).

Merchant traders waiting for their ship to come in.

Mr. Micawber waiting for "something to turn up."

Lord Reith, the founder of the BBC, says that he spent virtually the entire period of World War II by the telephone, waiting for Winston Churchill to call him. He never did.

And think of all the little people waiting today—at the airport, at the bus depot, at the doctor's, at the amusement park, at the bowling alley, at the post office, the ticket office, the unemployment office, the Social Security office. Society has become a vast waiting room.

"Waiting for Lefty" was a controversial Broadway play by Clifford Odets. "Lefty" is a labor leader who is expected by the rank and file to lead a strike that will uphold the cause of suffering humanity against the capitalistic bosses.

If history teaches anything, it teaches that people will wait for "Lefty," and he will come, and then they will wait for someone to deliver them from "Lefty".

"Waiting for Godot" is a totally different kind of drama by Samuel Beckett. Four wretched characters, utterly lost in the meaninglessness of their lives, keep waiting for someone named Godot to rescue them. No one knows who Godot is or when he will come. He seems to be someone very much like God. He never appears.

The play's message is clear: waiting for Godot is useless because there is no Godot. Just so, waiting for God is futile.

But is it?

It is certainly true that we cannot at the same time be waiting for God and waiting for man. That was my problem: I pretended to be a son of Mary, but actually I was a son of Martha in a clerical collar.

But waiting for God is not like waiting for Godot. It is not like Lord Reith waiting for Churchill to offer him an important wartime position. The Bible so testifies in a thousand places; and if you try it, your own experience will prove it.

When Andrew Murray, the South African pastor and author, faced a crisis in his personal life, he took it to the Lord. As he waited upon God he thought:

> First of all, God brought me here; it is by his will that I am in this strait place: in that fact I will rest. Next, he will keep me here in his love, and give me grace to behave as his child. Then, he will make the trial a blessing, teaching me the lessons he intends me to learn, and working in me the grace he means to bestow. Last, in his good time, he can bring me out again—how and when, he knows. So I am here by God's appointment, in his keeping, under his training, for his time.*

On a single day in 1963 two serious blows afflicted members of my family. I drove around town with tears rolling down my cheeks, unaware that I was crying. But in that time of trauma one Bible verse stayed with me moment by moment: "Then the devil leaveth him, and behold! Angels came and ministered unto him" (Matthew 4:11).

I waited for the angels, and they came. When we wait for the things of God, he responds. When we wait for the world, it's a long wait.

---

* *Decision*, (April 1961), p. 15. ©1961 by the Billy Graham Evangelistic Association. Reprinted by permission.

WHEN?

Well, Father, here I am.

Yes.

I'm waiting, Father.

Quite so.

Aren't You going to do anything?

What do you wish done?

I want to be filled with Your Spirit.

You are certain of this?

Of course. I want it all: the filling, the baptism, the fire, the anointing, the indwelling, the gifts, the fruit—the whole package.

You aim high.

Everything's set, Father; the ball is in Your court.

How is everything set?

I mean I've done everything I was supposed to do. I've humbled myself, and prayed, and sought Your face, and turned from my old bad ways.

And . . .

Now I'm waiting on You.

Good.

But I don't want to wait. At least, not for long. Look, I'm young, full of life. I want to see some glory and excitement right now. I don't have forever, Lord.

But I do.

Yes, but You're different. I'm . . .

Yes?

I'm involved in a lot of things: projects, programs, deadlines, people expecting me here and there. My schedule is full, Father.

Then why are you here?

I thought I explained that. I want to be filled with Your

Spirit. The pressure of these responsibilities is getting too great. I need help.

Yes, you do.

Seems like when I first came to Jesus, Your Spirit was more in control of me than he is now.

What happened?

You know what happened. My ego took a trip.

True.

The power couldn't get through; the way was blocked. So now I've been to the cross, and have asked You to take myself out of the way, and make me lovable, and all that.

Good.

And here I am.

Yes.

Father, are You putting me on?

Explain yourself.

You're stalling.

No. You are stalling.

I'm waiting to be filled with Your Spirit. That's what's on my mind, and it's the only thing on my mind.

Then wait, my child.

But how long? Till I drop?

Simeon waited.

Who?

Simeon.

You mean that old man in the Temple when they brought the baby Jesus?

Yes. He waited a lifetime. Jacob waited. Hannah waited. David waited.

Father, what are the logistics of waiting? Is there something I'm supposed to be doing while I wait?

You have not even begun to wait.

Begun? Seems as if I've been here for hours.

But you have not been waiting.
What have I been doing?
Fidgeting. Squirming. Complaining.
All right, I'll close my eyes and go limp.
Fine.
I may go to sleep.
Excellent.
I don't have to remind You that the devil isn't asleep, Father. He is fierce and active, and tearing up the place. I think he's getting ready to finish off the human race.
Do you wish to engage him in combat?
No, I want to be filled with Your Spirit so that You will engage him in combat. I know perfectly well I can't fight him in my own strength. So we'd better get on with it, don't You think? It isn't that I mind waiting; I'm just not much on techniques of meditation. The contemplative life of a mystic is not for me.
Get on with what?
Father, if You're going to do something, do it.
What do you wish done?
Rev me up. Set me going. Give me the Holy Spirit. My tank's gone dry.
Oh, no, it has not.
You mean there's some fuel in the bottom?
Too much.
How can I get rid of it?
By my Spirit.
But when? When? When?
Wait.

THE DEVIL'S POSTPILE

The history of revival teaches us that there *is* something we can do while we wait. Not that it will have the slightest effect one way or the other on the filling of the Spirit. But it needs to be done.

When revival came to Ebenezer Baptist Church in Saskatoon, Saskatchewan, in the fall of 1971, many of the people set about making amends. As Leonard Ravenhill wrote in his letter, articles were returned to shops, accounts were put straight, words of healing passed between members of families.

In a neighboring city the pastor of a church was vexed by three complex problems in human relations, as he later described them to me. One involved a difference between two grandmothers; another concerned a husband and wife; and still another entailed a business partnership. The upshot was that some of his church members were not speaking to each other.

When the Sutera brothers brought their crusade to that city, the pastor was astonished to find all three problems being resolved at the foot of the cross.

"If you are standing before the altar in the Temple, offering a sacrifice to God," said Jesus, "and suddenly remember that a friend has something against you, leave your sacrifice there beside the altar and go and apologize and be reconciled to him, and then come and offer your sacrifice to God" (Matt. 5:24, Living Bible).

Waiting is a time of reflection. It may be that a debt needs to be settled. Or possibly just a visit is needed, or a telephone call, or a letter. Or something altogether different may be required. It's enough that God knows about it and that you intend to do something about it.

The beautiful part is that when we set about to make things right, help comes from beyond ourselves. God sends a supernatural infusion of divine love to enable us to do it. As John says, "If we love one another, God abides in us, and his love is completed in us" (1 John 4:12).

It's incredible, really, how we manage to make a mess of things. In fact it's funny. We set out to do a Christian deed with the best of good will, and find ourselves shot down in flames.

For example, we make an earnest effort at witnessing for Christ and end by doing more harm than good. ("Want to know what I think of your Christianity? It's phony!")

We perform an unselfish act at considerable inconvenience to ourselves and it is promptly interpreted as selfishness on our part. ("You and your Lady Bountiful image—you make me sick.")

We share with some church members a bit of Christian teaching that helped us over some rough spots, and have our ears boxed for daring to speak up. ("I don't know where you're getting this stuff, but I wish you'd keep it to yourself.")

We show the kindest of intentions toward someone, but our approach is misconstrued as an unfriendly gesture. ("Save your advice for someone who asks you for it.")

We bestow a generous gift and are rebuked because it isn't more. ("Thanks for the check. I hope it didn't break up your business.")

So we draw back hurt, and build a fence against the person who was unkind, and as time passes our feelings congeal and harden. The preacher preaches about love, but it never reaches us. We'll love, all right, but to avoid future hurts we intend to be selective about it.

Now who needs to be filled with the Spirit?

What happened in little churches in Saskatchewan, Alberta, Manitoba, and British Columbia was that people began forgiving each other. Some of them hadn't spoken to each other in years. They found out that where restitution is concerned, forgiveness is a two-way street. Not only did they need to be forgiven, they needed to forgive.

But forgiveness is a word that people don't like very well, and with good reason. It seems to turn everything into mush. We can forgive a child for swinging a cat by the tail, but when we get into more serious things, forgiveness seems to imply that wrongdoing doesn't really matter that much.

That is where the Gospel reveals its divine character. In the Bible forgiveness always has a price tag on it. Without the shedding of blood there is no remission of sins (cf. Heb. 9:22). It cost the blood of his Son for God to forgive the world its behavior. Our guilt was laid on the guiltless Savior, which is why every day of their lives Christians thank God for Jesus Christ.

But Christians who decide to forgive usually have to swallow a lot of painful memories. It's not just a matter of returning a "liberated" umbrella to the department store, or coughing up some conscience money. Forgiveness is much more galling. We Christians have to see ourselves as sinners saved by grace, but mired in self-love, resentment, and fear. We have to face the fact that we too were wrong; that to be honest we are no better than anyone else.

> If you feel inclined to set yourself up as a judge of those who sin, let me assure you, whoever you are, that you are in no position to do so. For at whatever point you condemn others you automatically condemn yourself, since you, the judge, commit the same sins (Rom 2:1, Phillips).

So what do we do? We wait at Calvary; and as we wait, we reflect about certain people in our lives, and we say the words we heard from Jesus: "Father, forgive . . ."

High in the California Sierras rises a strange formation known as the Devil's Postpile. At its base lies an amorphous mass of scree and loose rock, stacked in a most disordered way. It occurs to me that it would make an appropriate dumping ground for the bad memories of Christians. If we could toss our hurts and grudges there and let the snow cover them, what a blessing it would be.

In a sense Jesus Christ covered our memories of the past through his atoning death on the cross. "God," Billy Graham once said, "has erased my sins from his memory as a tape recorder erases its sound track."

The miracle of the new birth is that by grace (and only by grace) we can say to the person who has put us through a bad scene, "Forget it. Let's start over." We can even laugh about it. Professor Gordon Allport, the psychologist, says that "a case might be made for the potentially superior humor" of the person "who has settled once and for all what things are of ultimate value, sacred and untouchable. For then nothing else in the world need be taken seriously."[*]

So we laugh, because we see that the problem we had with someone else had its absurd and niggling elements. And in the laughter our magnanimity surfaces—and that is the greatest restitution of all.

But is the activity we have been describing just another kind of moral muscle or strenuous sainthood? A disguised way of earning our salvation and letting "good works" in at the back door? God forbid. It rather is a quiet setting of our house in order so that when and if God commands the blessing in our direction, we will be ready and waiting.

THE APPOINTED HOUR

You are a guest in a gracious home, and the members of the household have gone out and left you alone in the living room. You sit in an easy chair reading a book. All is quiet. After a while, much to your surprise, the family tabby cat pads over, leaps into your lap, and settles down with a purr, ready to love and be loved.

---

[*] Gordon Allport, *Personality: A Psychological Interpretation* (New York: Holt, 1937).

What better way to describe the working of the Holy Spirit? We sit quietly and wait, at peace, not even knowing fully what we are waiting for, and he comes. Gently, unobtrusively, he makes known his loving Presence.

We might have imagined that God would manifest his Spirit to us by means of his divine might and glory, with tongues of flame, rushing winds, and all the rest. After all it did happen once, and people still have visions; why not us? But as Phillips Brooks suggests in his well-loved hymn, "O Little Town of Bethlehem," God seems to work differently in his ordinary children's lives from the spectacular way he works in the rest of his creation:

> How silently, how silently,
>   the wondrous gift is given;
> So God imparts to human hearts
>   the blessings of his heaven.

In recent years, as I have related, I have engaged with friends in visiting churches at their invitation and conducting evening prayer circles. The only unusual aspect of these circles is that we kneel and pray for each other. Winola has often joined me in these prayer times. Only rarely has God seemed to provide an immediate, supernatural answer to prayer at such gatherings. Usually it is a matter of asking and waiting.

One particular Afterglow the people nicknamed "Prayer on the Rocks," since they gathered late in the evening in what used to be a fishpond. We received a letter from a woman who attended an Afterglow in this place. She had asked for prayer concerning a difficult family situation. A month later she wrote us:

> What a victory that was—and still is. I had been carrying that burden around on my heart for three long, heavy years, with the tears ready to overflow at any time; and always there was the ache. I was eager and willing to commit the burden to the Lord and

knew he was most willing to take it from me, but it seemed that the harder I tried to commit it, the harder it came back. It was as though a great dome of glass was covering me, cutting me off from God.

It wasn't until we got down to business in prayer on the rocks, and all the dear ones joined me and actually touched me, that the breakthrough came. *I didn't feel that night that anything particular had happened,* except I now had a great desire to pray with and for the others and their burdens.

But the next morning I suddenly realized that the ache and the burden were gone and they have been gone ever since. There isn't a single tear anywhere near the surface. When others get upset about the situation I feel calm, peaceful, relaxed, and just plain happy. In short, prayer on the rocks worked (Used by permission).

This woman's time of waiting was short, and much of it was filled with prayer and love for others. Why was it short? God moves in mysterious ways beyond our fathoming. His timing is not the same as ours. He is not listening to a different drummer, he *is* the different Drummer—which makes our waiting a vital part of the Gospel message.

We who like immediate returns and daily interest on our investments may not be enchanted with the idea of an indeterminate delay, but there it is. God says "Yes," he says "No," or he says "Wait." For a Christian there is no unanswered prayer.

For verification, consider the importance of waiting in these scriptural promises, first in the Old Testament:

Wait on the Lord; be of good courage, and he shall strengthen thine heart: wait, I say, on the Lord (Ps. 27:14).

Those that wait upon the Lord, they shall inherit the earth (Ps. 37:9).

I waited patiently for the Lord, and he inclined unto me (Ps. 40:1).

My soul, wait thou only upon God; for my expectation is from him (Ps. 62:5).

They that wait upon the Lord shall renew their strength; they shall mount up with wings as eagles. (Is. 40:31).

And it shall come to pass afterward, that I will pour out my Spirit on all flesh (Joel 2:28).

And in the New Testament:

Eye hath not seen, nor ear heard, neither have entered into the heart of man, the things which God hath prepared for them that love him (1 Cor. 2:9).

He charged them . . . to wait for the promise of the Father, which, he said, "you heard from me, for John baptized with water, but before many days you shall be baptized with the Holy Spirit" (Acts 1:4-6, RSV).

A most intriguing passage in the prophecy of Isaiah (30:18) suggests that the reason for the Lord's delay in meeting human need is that he is piling up the blessing: "And therefore will the Lord wait, that he might be gracious unto you." For sheer beauty of expression, however, I believe the best word on this subject is to be found in Moffatt's translation of Habakkuk 2:3 in these magnificent lines:

The vision has its own appointed hour,
it ripens, it will flower;
if it be long, then wait,
for it is sure, and it will not be late.

5. Filling

> The Spirit of the Lord is upon me; because the Lord has anointed me . . . to give . . . beauty for ashes, the oil of joy for mourning, the garment of praise for the spirit of heaviness . . . (Isa. 61:1,3).

So now it has happened. The Comforter has come, as Jesus said he would. Those beautiful words uttered by Isaish so long ago have become ours.

What we hoped and longed for has come to pass. In some mysterious way our head has been anointed with the oil of joy. The blessing has arrived—heaped up, pressed down, shaken together, running over. At his own pleasure, in the serene majesty of his glorious Person, God has acted.

Our Lord Jesus Christ has revealed his truth through his Word; we have heard, believed, and accepted it; our prayers and honest confessions have been received at the throne of heaven; the crucifixion of the self has become a personal reality; and the waiting time has come to an end.

All we can say is, "Hallelujah! Praise the Lord!"

I have written barely 150 words of this chapter, and already many readers are mystified. They are asking, "What is he talking about? Whose blessing? What happened anyway?"

Well, as a working journalist trained in the old "green eyeshade school," I feel they are entitled to know. My approach to a news story is still based on Who? What? When? Where? How? and Why? And since the filling of the Spirit is one of the great stories of human history, I'm giving it the treatment.

WHO?

Why, God, of course. He does it all. He does it as God the Father, God the Son, God the Holy Spirit: the Triune God. We initiate nothing. God acts; we react. Whether we are speaking of personal renewal or revival in the church, God does it or it isn't done. Even our warped and finite minds can understand that much.

We can read our Bibles until they fall apart, but God's Spirit has to breathe through the words or they remain just that— words. We can erect million-dollar cups and saucers to catch the Living Water, but until the Spirit fills them they remain monuments to our own generation.

WHAT?

Just this: the love of God is poured out into our hearts by the Holy Spirit. Nothing covert, nothing esoteric, but the whole experience supernatural. We who once were occupied— if not obsessed—with the claims of self are now filled with the Spirit of the Living God.

We used to resent people, envy people, fear people, shun people, even detest and despise people. Now God has filled us with love for them. His perfect love has cast out our fears and our bitterness. His Spirit has warmed the temperature of human relations, has replaced aloofness with good feeling. Our lives are flooded with peace and joy, but most of all with love.

The same love that caused Jesus Christ to go to the cross for us, and to send us the Spirit of Truth, now motivates us to reach out to others. We want to help people if we can do it without getting in the way and making nuisances of ourselves.

You understand that we had nothing to do with this change except to ask for it. No matter how badly we might have wanted it, we couldn't have brought it about. Our good resolutions would crack up every time. We're too human. But God is God, and when he moves, he moves in sovereignty. He sends no envoys or plenipotentiaries, he comes himself. He says to his church, "You have been sweeping things under the rug. I am pulling back the rug." He says to his child, "My finger is pointed at you. I am redesigning your behavior pattern."

And who can stand before the Lord? When he tells us to love each other, we respond or face the grave consequences.

WHEN?

The Biblical statement is that God moves "in the fulness of time." That is to say, he acts when he is ready. He responds to our prayer that we might be filled with his Spirit, but he keeps his own schedule. Since he is Lord of time, we adjust our convenience and expectation to his good pleasure.

The question persists, are we speaking now of God's action at our conversion or at some later date? Is the filling of the Spirit a first blessing, a second blessing, or a whole series of blessings?

The New Testament is quite clear that no one comes to Jesus Christ unless the Spirit draws him. All the attributes of Deity, all the power and glory, all the angels of heaven are present when a sinner repents and is saved.

Some students of the Bible have informed me that once the Holy Spirit takes control of a believer's life, he stays in control. That was my position after becoming a Christian, and in a sense I still maintain it to be true. Yet I must admit today that it is possible to be an active, practicing, Bible-loving, Christ-honoring Christian and not to be filled with the Spirit and with love, because for years that was precisely my condition.

I loved Jesus! I loved to think about him and sing about him! But I was frustrated, like a sports car I once observed during an Arizona flood, trying to cross a railroad bridge on the ties.

The Apostle Paul tells us, "Be filled with the Spirit." He doesn't say when or how frequently. For many it has never happened at all. Try it for size; if it fits, wear it.

WHERE?

It could happen anywhere. William Camden wrote in 1605, "Betwixt the stirrup and the ground/Mercy I asked, mercy I found."

I was sitting in front of my television set a few days after that January "Afterglow" when it occurred to me that something wonderful had taken its place. But it could happen to someone while praying in church, or while munching a jumbo hamburger, or while soaring in the middle of a hang-glider flight. It could happen quite gradually over a period of time. God reaches out and touches us and we are filled with his Spirit.

HOW?

How indeed! We know that the Holy Spirit loves a vacuum, but to ask just how God goes about filling people with love is to brush up against a mystery that only heaven will reveal.

WHY?

"He shall not speak of himself but . . . he shall glorify me" (John 16:13-14). Thus did Jesus describe the work of the Holy Spirit.

In the early years of this century a remarkable man of God named Samuel Zeller conducted a "spiritual sanitorium" at Männedorf on the shore of Lake Zürich, Switzerland. Zeller was known for his ministry of prayer; and yet it was said of him that "after all he prays only one prayer, namely, that the name of God might be glorified."*

When we ask the question, "Why has God chosen to fill us with his Spirit?" our answer can only be "to glorify himself." Nothing else suits our case.

We may look for other ways in which we might glorify God—by deeding a piece of property, perhaps, or writing a hymn, or putting up a temple. But Jesus said that the one truly acceptable way to give glory to his Father was for us to treat each other with love. And it was to fill us with that love that he sent his Spirit.

Not to make me bubbly and exuberant.

Not to set an example of my good behavior.

Not to prove that Christians are happier than anybody else.

Not to bring about world peace.

But to make me a loving person whose love would glorify the God of love.

THE CATALYST

For years my mother-in-law was an enigma to me. Her zeal presented no difficulty; I understood her motives. To be candid, living under the same roof and being uneasily aware that she wanted me converted, I was inclined to be nasty. When she fixed her bifocals on me and announced, "Sherwood, you need to be born again," I would come back with, "Why? So I can be like you?"

But there was something about Mother Wells that had me

---

* Hallesby, p. 126.

mystified, and that something was her ability to love. She had no business loving me the way she did.

Faith McCain Wells was a small woman. Winola says that when she was a child and heard the Bible expression, "O ye of little faith," she always thought that Jesus was speaking to her. Although Faith was diminutive, gentle, and (most of the time) reticent, when she stood before a class with a Bible in her hand she became a tiger. Under her exposition the notes in the Scofield Reference Edition of the Holy Bible assumed almost a supernatural authority.

Yet neither her zeal nor her doctrine explained her love. Well-trained in the Bible, Mother Wells disagreed with much, if not most, of what I was being taught in seminary. (I was one of those well-meaning, unregenerate, bewildered misfits who find themselves studying for the ministry without knowing why.) She knew that her daughter faced a dubious future married to a theological risk. (Furthermore, she knew that I was thirty years old and broke.)

She loved to talk about the blood of Christ and the miracle of the resurrection, and she made a rather large point of repentance. "Sherwood," she would say, "never stand in the pulpit without mentioning our Lord's atonement for our sins."

Her favorite subject was prophecy and the end of the world. Of all the books of the Bible, she preferred to discuss Daniel and Revelation. Since Mother Wells' homegoing in 1961 I have missed the tiptoe expectation that marked her teaching.

If neither her zeal nor her doctrine resolved her mystery, neither did her discipline, although she had a regimen I have often coveted. Each night after dinner we had devotions and Bible reading. Then on Sundays the parade of radio programs would start as soon as we returned from church. First, Percy Crawford and the "Young People's Church of the Air," then Dr. DeHaan's "Radio Bible Class," followed by "Brother Fuller" and the "Old Fashioned Revival Hour," and "First Mate

Bob" and the "Crew of the Good Ship Grace." She would wind up with Walter Maier and the "Lutheran Hour," Dr. Harry Ironside, Dr. Donald Grey Barnhouse, or Mr. Arnold Grunigen.

The radio volume was turned up so that I could hear it in my study, where I was absorbing a textbook dedicated to the proposition that John couldn't have written John because someone else named John got there first and siphoned off the market.

In spite of the unpromising image I presented, Mother Wells believed in me, showered me with affection, prayed for me, and instructed me whenever I would let her.

In the providence of God, the time arrived when I began to adopt her beliefs. Instead of arguing with her, I would listen to her. I knew she had something that I lacked as I attempted to preach on weekends in a country church on the shore of San Francisco bay. (My sermons could be summed up in four words: "Let us all behave." But my sparse congregation consisted of persons who were already behaving better than I.)

When I finally abandoned the shipwreck of my floundering spiritual life and was washed ashore on a beach called Jesus, she didn't seem at all surprised. I was the one who gaped in astonishment.

Her discipline hadn't reached me any more than her zeal or her doctrine had. Only her love got through to me, and it has taken years for me to understand the source of Mother Wells' love. I now know it was the Holy Spirit.

I recall clearly from my student days her teaching about the Third Person of the Trinity, because she spoke of him so often and my teachers mentioned him so seldom. The working of the Holy Spirit in the life of the believer, she explained, was made evident in the fruit of the Spirit.

But she repudiated David's prayer in the fifty-first Psalm ("Take not thy Holy Spirit from me") and refused to repeat it because, she said, that prayer belonged to a former age. She maintained that the Holy Spirit, given to the church at Pentecost, would never be taken away until Jesus returned.

Today Mother Wells is an enigma no longer. I realize that she loved me in spite of my poor qualities and dim prospects, not because she was a skilled Bible teacher but because she was a Spirit-filled woman. In the richness of his grace and in response to her prayer, the Spirit of God had given her a supernatural love for her son-in-law.

Harry Thiessen once said to me, "Heaven is full of answers to prayer that have never been claimed." Mother Wells put in a claim for me. I believe that thanks to her prayers and her love, I'll see her in Heaven.

ACCEPTANCE AND OPENNESS

George Santayana, the Italian-American philosopher poet, has left us a moving description of an evangelical friend and school chum whom he knew when he lived in Boston.

After describing the dominant trait in his friend as "clear goodness," Santayana writes, "He delighted in pleasant ways and people. Love of historic Christianity opened to him a wonderful world existing before and beyond America. He felt at home in the church. He was civilized. . . ."

Santayana then asks a question:

Why did a strictly Puritan and inward religion in him, far from producing narrowness or fanaticism, produce charity and hospitality of mind? Not that he was in the least what was called liberal, that is, indifferent and vaguely contemptuous toward all definite doctrines or practices, and without any discipline of his own.

On the contrary he was absolutely loyal to his own tradition, and master of it; he was made, finished, imposing in the precision of his affections. He had perfect integrity, yet he had sweetness, too, affection for what he excluded from his own sphere, justice to what he renounced, happiness in the joys of others that were not joys to him, so that his very limitations were turned into admirable virtues.

Here was this manly boy . . . firmly and contentedly rooted . . . yet accepting, respecting, and even envying me for being everything that he was not and did not expect to be.*

Santayana's young friend beautifully illustrates the liberating effect of the Holy Spirit upon a Christian's relationships with other people: "Charity and hospitality of mind . . . perfect integrity, yet sweetness . . . justice to what he renounced . . . firmly rooted, yet respecting."

In his ministry of glorifying Jesus Christ, the Holy Spirit teaches us to separate ourselves from sin but not from the sinner. The last thing Christ wants us to do is to withdraw from other people ["Go ye into the world" (Mark 16:15)]. He wants us to join the human race but not to become one of its victims.

Today the evangelical community is recognizing as never before that acceptance and openness are indispensable to its witness in the name of Jesus Christ. Love never compromises New Testament theology or moral standards. But when we become appreciative and loving, our testimony to the Gospel is established upon an effective base.

To be filled with the Spirit is not to go around looking for people who are in a state of something less than blessedness, and either chopping them off or putting them down. We don't invite people to church by saying, "Maybe if you'd go to a church like ours, God wouldn't let you get all strung out like this!"

Rather our attitude is founded on the New Testament's teaching that "faith . . . worketh by love" (Gal. 5:6). It is more than tolerance. It is an application of our devotion to Jesus Christ, born out of our security in him and our assurance of his

---

* George Santayana, *Persons and Places* (New York: Scribner's, 1944), pp. 183-184.

salvation. Such devotion prevents us from becoming imperial-istic and arrogant about our Christianity, and thinking that we are better than other people.

C. S. Lewis said during my 1963 interview with him, "There are many different ways of bringing people into God's Kingdom, even some ways that I specially dislike. I have therefore learned to be cautious."

Christians have been known to say about some member of their immediate family, "I'd give anything to see him come to Christ." What does the New Testament say about it? Does it counsel, "Stuff your pocket full of tracts and and go after him"? Does it say, "Wither him with argument"? "Quote Scripture by the yard"? "Haul him to church"? "Send him a subscription to a religious magazine"? "Charter a Gospel blimp"?

No, it doesn't. What does it say?

It says, "Be filled with the Spirit" (Eph. 5:18). That's another way of saying (in this case), "Be filled with love for your relative and let the Spirit do his work."

On a number of occasions, Billy Graham has responded to individuals of another religious tradition. A young woman came forward during one of his crusade invitations and called to him out of the crowd. "Because of your appeal," she said, "I have decided to commit my life to Christ and become a nun."

Billy leaned over and said to her, "God bless you."

A Catholic bishop sat on the platform at a rally in a South American city. When people responded to the invitation, the bishop rose and began blessing them as they walked down the aisle. A committee member asked Mr. Graham to stop it. Mr. Graham's reply was, "He's your bishop. You stop him."

After a meeting in New York City, a young rabbi came to the platform and spoke to the evangelist. "What do you do with me?" he demanded. "Send me to hell because I'm a rabbi?"

Mr. Graham shook his hand warmly. "I congratulate you,"

he said. "To be a Jewish rabbi is a great honor and privilege. You and I disagree perhaps over the coming of the Messiah, but I have high respect for you, and thank God for you."

"Affection for what he excluded from his own sphere . . . happiness in the joys of others that were not joys to him, so that his very limitations were turned into admirable virtues . . ."

TURN HIM LOOSE

One of my favorite New Testament personalities is Lazarus. We know little about the man other than that he had two sisters, and he died, and Jesus raised him from the dead. What Lazarus accomplished for Christ is not recorded; what we are told is what Christ did for Lazarus.

The whole eleventh chapter of John is rich in spiritual teaching, but let's look specifically at the forty-fourth verse:

> And he who had been dead came forth, bound hand and foot with grave clothes, and his face bound about with a handkerchief. Jesus says to them, Loose him and let him go.

Here is the prototype of the Spirit-filled Christian. Lazarus is given no specific orders, he is simply turned loose in the world to be a follower of Jesus. He has no need to boast about what God has done for him; anyone can see that. Lazarus will witness to the miracle of the resurrection every time he walks down the street. So Jesus says, "Turn him loose."

But is there to be no plan for Lazarus' life? It is an interesting question. The specific word *plan* does not appear in the Bible. Neither does *scheme, strategy, program* or *schedule.* Instead we read of God's *purpose,* a much broader word and one rich in possibilities.

I don't know what orders Jesus gave to Lazarus apart from calling him back from the dead, but I do know his *purpose* in bringing about the miracle. It was not a public relations stunt. It was not a demonstration of his ability to reverse the processes of nature. It was not to prolong human life beyond its natural limits.

Jesus called back Lazarus from the grave to vindicate his testimony to Lazarus' sister Martha, "I am the resurrection, and the life: he that believeth in me, though he were dead, yet shall he live" (John 11:25). Samuel Chadwick, the British evangelist, declares in one of his books that people do not come to church to see Jesus; they come to see Lazarus. To behold death turned into life—whether it be spiritual or physical—is to behold in a magnificent way the purpose of God fulfilled on earth. The greatest story in literature ends with the words, "This thy brother was dead, and is alive again; and was lost, and is found" (Luke 15:32).

As for a plan, it could be said that Lazarus was given one after all. The closest word to *plan* in the New Testament is *predestinate*, which we are told actually means "to design or mark out beforehand." In Ephesians 1:11 Paul writes that Christians are "predestinated according to the purpose of him who works all things according to the counsel of his will, for us to be to the praise of his glory." F. F. Bruce, the British scholar, tells us that according to one interpretation of Romans 8:28, the Holy Spirit works for good in everything with those who love God. Certainly the Holy Spirit has blessed millions through the story of the raising of Lazarus. As Dostoevsky shows us in his stirring novel "Crime and Punishment," God's plan is much in evidence in this most famous of Jesus' mighty acts.

It must remain a mystery whether it was God's specific and detailed "plan" that some of his choicest servants should be subjected to barbaric cruelty, burned to death, drowned, gored, scalped, drawn and quartered, shot, eaten by cannibals, or brainwashed into idiocy. There are some things we will never understand in this life. But we can never question God's purpose, which is that we might be conformed to the image of his Son.

I wonder about Lazarus sometimes. I try to imagine what might have happened if someone other than Jesus, the sisters, and the professional mourners had been on hand when he came back from the grave. Had the coroner been there, he probably would have had a few things to say. The medical examiner might have had even more, considering the length of time Lazarus had spent in the tomb. The insurance adjuster, had he been present, would have had a few notes for his book. I can't conjecture what the television people would have done with the story.

But apart from the official people, plus the exploiters and the curious, undoubtedly there would have been some earnest Christians present who would want to protect Lazarus from the snares of that master planner, the devil.

The real effort of such "protection" might well have been to put Lazarus back in the cave where one could keep an eye on him. There he could have been encouraged to study the Bible, perhaps take a correspondence course, and get in touch with a good church school. He might even have taken up the guitar. Then when Lazarus was properly prepared, he could have begun to . . .

But Jesus said, "Loose him and let him go." He said, "The wind blows where it wills, and you hear its sound, but you do not know where it comes from or where it is going; thus is everyone who has been born of the Spirit" (John 11:44, 3:8).

Bible courses are vital; church institutions are indispensable; planning ahead is always wise. But to the Spirit-filled person life can no longer be reduced to a regimented, controlled procedure with a rigid calendar of action. The careful plans we make may well be the very grave clothes Jesus is telling us to unwind.

When the Holy Spirit takes over a life, he preempts the

field. His plan, his purpose, is to conform us to the image of
Jesus Christ. But he is love, and who can say what love will do?

THE SECRET OF EVANGELISM

Everybody wants love. The motorcyclist zipping between
cars, the cultist panhandling at the airport, the CIA secret
agent, the Mafia hit man, the burlesque chorine, the high-rise
janitor all want love. So do printers and plumbers and acrobats,
housewives and investment bankers.

Many of them are searching for it in the wrong places and
not finding it. They think that love will come by money, or by
sex, or by fame, or by learning, but they soon become disillu-
sioned. Some even look toward the church, for church people
talk a lot about love. But as often as not the searchers turn
away, saying, "I understand they're having some kind of
trouble. I guess there's no love there either."

Jesus did not die on the cross to make church members of
everybody. He died to save us from sin, death, and hell, and to
pour out the love of God into our hearts by his Spirit.

Evangelism—the effective spreading of the Good News—is
thus conditional upon a spiritual climate in the church that can
best be described as a state of renewal or revival. The alterna-
tive Jesus put in the form of a question: "Can the blind lead the
blind? Shall they not both fall into the ditch?" (Luke 6:39).

In his discourses and parables Jesus showed that he was
interested in more than the religious community, that his heart
reached out to human beings everywhere. "God so loved the
world . . ." To cultivate the same attitude in us, he arranged for
Pentecost. Jesus knew that once his Church was filled with the
Holy Spirit's love, it would have all the equipment it needed to
evangelize.

That's what evangelism is: people loving people into the
circle of God's love.

One of the great tragedies in evangelistic work is the fact that many of those who step forward at the invitation to make a commitment to Jesus Christ fail to connect with a local church.

The problem has been analyzed many times. Usually the fault is not attributed to the preaching message or to the preparation and follow-up activity. Instead, the failure is said to lie with the local church. Unless the church is Spirit-filled, it seems to lack the ability to attract, welcome, and absorb newly committed people.

What then are the marks of a Spirit-filled church? Let me mention five I have uncovered in the New Testament:

Prayer
Witnessing
Conversions
Joy
Love

Most Christians might agree with my list, but some would want to add certain other characteristics of the New Testament church they would link to the Holy Spirit. For example, they would include the preaching of the Word, fidelity to the Scriptures, orthodox doctrine, valid church leadership, correct ecclesiology, and proper administration of the sacraments and ordinances. I would be the last to say such matters are not important. They are vital.

But they are not always evidence of the presence of the Holy Spirit.

One can hand the bread and wine to a brother while loathing him. One can murmur "Amen" to a fine Gospel sermon while retaining all kinds of bitterness and prejudice within. One can serve four terms as a deacon and still act ugly around the house. It could be said that one could also pray without the Spirit and witness without the Spirit. (I ought to know, I did these things often enough.) The key here is effectiveness. Without the Spirit everything is like wading in molasses; with the Spirit there comes a quickening.

In many churches I daresay the Holy Spirit could tiptoe out the front door and he would not even be missed. Church suppers, board meetings, elections, and budget-raising would go on as usual.

But when the Spirit is present and is pouring out love— love between pastor and congregation, love between members, love between church people and strangers—then look for growth. Look for prayer, and joy, and witnessing, and conversions.

Why do you suppose people join churches? Notice that young couple walking in the door of your church, paying a first visit. What do you imagine they are looking for? A powerful sermon? Exalting music? Soft pews? A place to park the kids?

Wrong. They are looking for love. If they join your church, it is because they think they will find love there. Other considerations enter in, but love tops them all.

Now a year has passed, and the family is no longer visible. The church board goes over the roll and sadly removes the names. You murmur, "I guess they never had it in the first place."

Perhaps not. But my guess is that it was not a weak theology that caused the young couple to stop coming to church. They came looking for love and didn't find it.

Whenever true revival—that is, a revival of love—has taken place in church history, it has always led to evangelistic activity. It is one of the marks of revival that non-Christians are converted to Christ. Fill a church with love and the world will come knocking, for everyone wants love.

When the great revival broke out on the island of Hawaii in the year 1838 under the ministry of Titus Coan, on a single Sunday 1,705 persons joined the Hilo church.

Speaking of the present East Africa revival, Bishop Festo Kivengere has said, "We have never seen a condition when Christians are revived and people around them are not affected."

People, yes, all kinds of people, prostitutes and fishermen and tax collectors, acrobats and housewives and investment bankers. All looking for love.

What is the secret of evangelism? The filling of the Spirit.

CONTENTMENT

Contentment!

Beautiful, rare feeling.

The bitter taste of life, gone. The spirit of heaviness, the drag, the ratrace—all disappeared. The ego no longer clamoring for its place in the sun by trying to be the sun. The necessities of the moment reduced to their proper perspective.

The body under subjection. The mind fixed on Jesus.

The spirit freshened by the Spirit of God, ready to accept what comes, to mourn, to suffer, to laugh, to exult. The feeling that life is a positive value, that tomorrow is a pleasant prospect—not by virtue of circumstance but by the filling of the Holy Spirit.

The whole being tuned to the love of God and waiting for Jesus to come back.

I'm afraid that contentment does not score highly as an objective of common pursuit in our day. Even Christians fail to regard it as important. According to the opinion prevailing in some circles, true believers should be in a state of constant anguish and torment over the lost condition of humanity. If they are worth their salt, they should be on the battlefield, burning out for God, straining every muscle and nerve, reaching out beyond the ranges, and finally dying with their boots on.

How, one is asked, can the committed servant of Jesus Christ do anything else? One is reminded of the millions dying each year and passing into a Christless eternity; of Satan roaming the earth seeking whom he may devour; of the bloody confrontations shaping up in Asia and Africa; of the fact that "the night cometh when no man can work" (John 9:4).

And can we then sit at ease in Zion? Is not contentment the twin sister of complacency and the first cousin of sloth?

The difficulty is that so often the Christian's restless agitation actually hinders the spread of the Gospel. We're so evangelistic that we trip over our own feet. People fail to discover in us the calm demeanor of Jesus that the Gospel portraits show so clearly. They decide accordingly that our feverish promotional activities are not for Jesus at all, but for ourselves, that we might make ourselves great in heaven and rich on earth.

The Bible does not always applaud those obsessed by a hand-wringing sense of urgency. David did not compose the twenty-third Psalm on the dead run, while shuttling from one high-level conference to another. "I shall not want. . . . I shall fear no evil. . . . I shall dwell in the house of the Lord." These words breathe not impetuosity but contentment.

Buried in the Old Testament (2 Kings 4:8-37) is the story of a Shunnamite woman whose only child had died. The grief-stricken woman had befriended the prophet Elisha many times in the past; and following the tragedy she traveled the twenty-five miles to Mount Carmel to talk with the prophet. Elisha saw her coming far in the distance and sent his servant to greet her and to ask, "Is it well with you? Is it well with your husband? Is it well with the child?"

The Shunnamite woman answered, "It is well." What composure! What faith! And—what a reward was hers!

If we are to credit his own letters and the book of Acts, no one has yet outstripped the Apostle Paul in evangelistic zeal. No one ever longed more ardently than he to see souls brought to Christ. Yet Paul was a contented human being. He wrote to the church at Philippi, "I have learned, in whatever circumstances I am, to be content."

Content, while he clung for hours to a piece of wood in the middle of the Mediterranean sea. Content, while he yearned for the salvation of his kinsmen. Content with much or little, in freedom or in chains.

Here is the supreme benediction of the Holy Spirit's indwelling and filling. Compassion, understanding, helpfulness, those attitudes so characteristic of our Lord in his earthly ministry, become ours. We are allowed to adopt them, not stridently or officiously, but in a manner of life that is gentle, firm, and bannered with love.

We find ourselves not just living a life but having a ministry. We pray with Christians and God steps into their lives. We are given the unspeakable privilege of leading people to Jesus—yet are hardly aware of it.

What a way to spend our days! Whoever thought it would be like this?

We know from Scripture that special gifts and capabilities are given by the Spirit of God to individuals for use in building up the Body of Christ, the church. Tens of thousands of God's people have been blessed by such gifts. It is a subject that lies beyond the purview of this book.

But surely one gift of the heavenly Father is intended for *everyone* who has prepared his or her heart to receive it. It is the gift God wishes to impart to you. May you welcome it, enjoy it to the full, and pass it along.

The gift is contentment.

6. Epilogue

HOW TO BE FILLED WITH THE HOLY SPIRIT

1. Deal with your problem.
2. Ask God to crucify you.
3. Ask God to fill you with his Spirit.
4. Thank him for what he is going to do.